SHEPHERD'S GUIDE

50 Steps
with Jesus

Learning to Walk Daily With the Lord

DR. RON & MARSHA HARVELL
WITH WENDY K. WALTERS

DISCLAIMER: These 50 Steps are reflections of personal faith and do not represent the views of the Department of Defense or the United States Air Force.

Printed in the USA

Cover Design & Layout by Wendy K. Walters | www.wendykwalters.com
Wendy K. Walters was a contributing author for this project.

ISBN (Paperback): 978-1-7359477-0-9

Published By
Xaris Publications
Moncks Corner, South Carolina

Unless otherwise noted, Scripture quotations are taken from the *New American Standard Bible*®, Copyright © 1960, 1962, 1963, 1968, 1971, 1972, 1973, 1975, 1977, 1995 by The Lockman Foundation. Used by permission. www.Lockman.org

Portions of scripture taken from the *King James Version* are marked KJV. Originally published in 1611, this Bible is in the public domain.

For more information about this guide go to "The 50 Steps" section of our website, www.GodsGreaterGrace.com and click on the video, "Welcome to 50 STEPS WITH JESUS Learning To Walk Daily With The Lord."

To Contact the Authors:

www.GodsGreaterGrace.com

SHEPHERD'S NAME

_____

EMAIL ADDRESS

_____

TELEPHONE

_____

BELIEVER'S NAME

_____

EMAIL ADDRESS

_____

TELEPHONE

_____

*Jesus said, "I am the good shepherd, and I know My own
and My own know Me ..."*

—John 10:14

50 STEPS WITH JESUS

Learning to Walk Daily With the Lord

WELCOME

You are about to start a wonderful journey with the Lord. You may be a new believer or a believer who just wants to grow deeper in your relationship with God. You might be someone who is going to serve as a shepherd and will walk beside another believer in this journey, or you may be someone who is setting this ministry up for others. Whatever the case, we are excited you are about to grow in your relationship with Jesus and with other believers. May you fall more deeply in love with God as you discover how great His love is for you.

Listed below, you will find your starting place. For shepherds and ministry leaders, we encourage you to walk through the *50 Steps With Jesus New Believer's Guide* as well. Please feel free to print as many copies as you need for the purpose of teaching others how to walk with Jesus.

This is a gift from the Lord through us to you.

DR. RON AND MARSHA HARVELL

YOUR JOURNEY STARTS NOW!

NEW BELIEVER'S GUIDE:

The companion to this *50 Steps With Jesus Shepherd's Guide* is the *50 Steps With Jesus New Believer's Guide*. Please ensure that your students (or new believers) have their own copy of the *New Believer's Guide*, or that you are bringing the *New Believer's Guides* with you to your first meeting with them. This first meeting is called "Big Step 1."

SHEPHERD'S GUIDE

Jesus is the Good Shepherd, and throughout Scripture we are called His sheep or His lambs. Thank you for taking this great stride in the *50 Steps* ministry and following in the footsteps of Jesus by shepherding His flock. Throughout this guide, lambs will also be referred to as student, believer, and new believer. This is your guidebook. You will be using this manual in companionship with your students as they work through the *New Believer's Guide*. Your material begins on page 13.

MINISTRY LEADER'S GUIDE

For leaders of this *50 Steps* program, you can find ideas in Section 2, beginning on page 137 called "Ministry Leader's Guide." This will be very helpful in seeing how *50 Steps* works and how you can implement this tool throughout your church or ministry.

May the Lord richly bless you on each Step of your journey!

Learning to Walk Daily With the Lord

TOOLS FOR THE SHEPHERD

YOUR JOURNEY MAP

*Be on guard for yourselves and for all the flock, among which
the Holy Spirit has made you overseers, to shepherd the church
of God which He purchased with His own blood.*

—Acts 20:28

MINISTRY LEADER'S GUIDE

Therefore, you shall keep the commandments of the LORD your
God, to walk in His ways and to fear Him.

—Deuteronomy 8:6

PART ONE

TOOLS FOR THE SHEPHERD

Know that the LORD Himself is God;
It is He who has made us, and not we ourselves;
We are His people and the sheep of His pasture.

PSALM 100:3

THE ADVENTURE BEGINS

Welcome, Lamb Shepherd, to a journey with the Lord and with a new believer that promises to be one of the most rewarding times of your life. It is a glorious trip that you are about to embark upon!

Jesus will be helping you shape a new believer's entire Christian life. Ask the Lord to use the Holy Spirit to empower you on this 50 Step walk of discovery to help nourish His newly born lamb.

You and the Lord will walk together helping this lamb to:

*Today you embark
on a glorious trip!*

- know and love Jesus,

- be conversational in prayer,

- be able to study God's Word,

- and be an active part of your local church.

Your lamb will be taking their first steps as they learn to walk with Jesus.

As you begin, pause to pray and ask God to help you be in tune with Him and faithful to help tend your lamb. Ask God to help your lamb to grow deeply in love with Jesus.

<hr/>

THE PURPOSE OF 50 STEPS

The *50 Steps* journey will help any believer develop their relationship with the Lord and strengthen the foundations of their faith. A new believer will be able to grow from the very first day they become a Christian. As they grow, they will develop a solid understanding of who God is, and who they are in Him.

As a faithful shepherd, you will serve them by guiding them as they learn the simple and elementary things of faith. This learning goes beyond understanding truths and practices of Christianity; it touches the most important part of their Christian life—their personal relationship with the Trinity: God, Jesus Christ, and the Holy Spirit.

This **relationship** is the reason:

- God made them …

- Jesus died for them …

- the Holy Spirit lives inside of them!

Learning to Walk Daily With the Lord

Learning to walk with Jesus, their Great Shepherd, will help them understand, for the rest of their lives, the glorious greatness of the Christian life!

As a new believer, all of these wonderful truths may be overwhelming; therefore, *50 Steps* starts with the assumption that the student has no background in the faith. Each lesson is written as if the student did not know how to pray, or have any idea there was a book called the Bible, or know what a church family does.

For example, the early steps provide passages of Scripture that are written out in the guide for them. Some who use this guide may not have a Bible yet or be able to have one in their circumstances. As you journey with them, they will learn about the Bible, and then they will be able to look up verses on their own. Therefore, simplicity is good as they start out so they do not get frustrated. The same need for your gentle leadership in the Word is true for prayer and church life. From day one, you will be able to help them pray, know the Word, and be a part of the body of Christ!

While this guide is designed for new believers and those young in their faith, it is also a great faith rejuvenator for mature believers. In one life group who tested *50 Steps*, the group average for being a Christian was over 50 years. They shepherded one another through this journey and asked for more material like this *50 Steps* guide for them to use. The group loved how it drew them closer together. They had a marvelous time of personal growth and growing as a church family. In the review of the program, they all said the same thing throughout each week: "I wish I had gone through this as a new believer. It would have made such a difference in my life." One man said, "If I had known this information for how to walk with Jesus when I was 18, I would not have wasted 20 years of my life."

One lady from the life group shepherded a younger friend who was struggling with drug addiction. By using the *50 Steps,* the Lord turned her life around.

As you shepherd your new believer or one another, you will see God work through you in their lives. You fulfill a command of the Lord to feed His lambs!

"If I had known this information for how to walk with Jesus when I was 18, I would not have wasted 20 years of my life."

THE GREAT SHEPHERD'S COMMAND TO YOU

For your encouragement on this shepherding journey, hear the Lord speaking to you about the importance of feeding new lambs! The Bible passage which follows is from a conversation that the resurrected Jesus had with Peter on the shore of the Sea of Galilee. As you read the Scriptures, take note of what Jesus is saying to Peter, for it is vital to understand Jesus' heart at this crucial time. This conversation with Peter takes place after Peter denied Jesus three times on the day Jesus was crucified. Soon after this, Jesus ascended into Heaven.

Ten days after the ascension of Jesus at Pentecost in Jerusalem, the Holy Spirit began the church by making Christians out of those who believed. Jesus needed Peter and the rest of His followers to be ready to help the new believers grow. John recorded this important conversation when Peter was restored by Jesus. It is the Great Commission from the Gospel of John.

The Great Commission from John 21:15-17

Jesus restored Peter with His three questions about Peter's love for Him. Jesus, the Great Shepherd, followed each response from Peter with a command to carry on His shepherding ministry. In the dialogue, the words for "tend" and "shepherd" are different. The word "tend" means to feed or nourish.

Jesus' Commands to Peter (John 21:15-17)

*15So when they had finished breakfast, Jesus said to Simon Peter,
"Simon, son of John, do you love Me more than these?"*

He said to Him, "Yes, Lord; You know that I love You."

*He said to him, "**Tend My lambs**."*

*16He said to him again a second time,
"Simon, son of John, do you love Me?"*

He said to Him, "Yes, Lord; You know that I love You."

*He said to him, "**Shepherd My sheep**."*

17He said to him the third time, "Simon, son of John, do you love Me?"

*Peter was grieved because He said to him the third time,
"Do you love Me?"*

*And he said to Him, "Lord, You know all things;
You know that I love You."*

*Jesus said to him, "**Tend My sheep**."*

Imagine Jesus saying this to you, "Tend my lambs." It is a special honor to be with new believers at the beginning of their walks with Jesus. What an honor to be a part of tending His lambs!

You are fulfilling this commandment by caring for new believers in this *50 Steps* ministry. You are feeding and tending the new lambs. Just like for any new living being, that early nourishment ought to be daily. Therefore, the ministry of tending your lambs ought to be with daily food. The next section will help you be a good shepherd for your lamb.

BEING A GOOD LAMB SHEPHERD:

Here are some ideas for helping your new lamb be successful!

Be Prayerful for Your Lamb

- Pray because this is the Lord's work! Ask the Holy Spirit to give you the power to lead and feed your lamb and for the success of your lamb's growth.

- Remain prayerful for God's work in their lives every day.

Be Faithful to Your Lamb

- Finish all *50 Steps* with them. For many, this ministry is their first *50 Steps* of faith following salvation.

- Purposefully keep your eyes on the prize. The goals are to help new believers grasp God's love, walk with their Lord Jesus, and mature in faith.

Be Fruitful with Your Lamb

- Have daily contact with your lamb. A wonderful part of this ministry is that it requires an ongoing contact with the lamb and the lamb shepherd for all 50 Steps. This daily contact has proven to be vitally important to the believer. They look forward to it because it shows they are not alone, that you have expectations for them, and they can ask you questions.

- Meet face-to-face, ideally at least once a week. This face-to-face meeting is called a "Big Step." Daily steps are the other six lessons for the rest of the week. You will agree with your lamb on a way to make contact every day. The section below provides more ideas and specifics on how to shepherd your lamb.

SHEPHERD PREPARATION FOR EACH DAY

We wanted you to have ideas to help you on your journey! This section:

- **Principles for Meetings**

- **Ideas for Big Step Weekly Meetings**

- **Ideas for Daily Steps Encouragement**

- **Getting Ready for Big Step 1**

Principles for Meetings:

Daily contact is daily spiritual food for your lamb. It feeds them, motivates them, and gives them opportunities to ask questions each day rather than waiting for Big Step days.

Go through the lesson for yourself prior to contacting your lamb. You are encouraged to try doing the lesson prior to looking at your Journey Guide's answers.

Say or write support for your student along the lines of, "I am proud of you." "I am praying for you." "Do you have any questions?"

If your lamb asks you about something that you do not know, simply say, "I am not sure, but I will find out for you." Then contact your church or ministry's point of contact to ask them.

Be an encourager when ideas come up or mistakes are made. Imagine your lamb as one who is young in the faith and one who will make mistakes as they learn to walk with Jesus.

Most of the Scriptures printed in the guide are from The New American Standard Version. You or your church can swap them out to another translation if you prefer to do so.

The student may have a Bible with a different translation. They can use it for memory verses if they like and if your church has no issues with it.

Many who have memorized Scriptures found value in using index cards to memorize their verses. You can show them Step 27 in advance for techniques for memorizing Scripture. The chart below is the list for the entire 7 weeks.

WEEK ONE	Psalm 1:2-3
WEEK TWO	John 14:15, 21
WEEK THREE	Matthew 6:9-13 (Optional 1 John 1:9)
WEEK FOUR	2 Timothy 3:16; Psalm 1:1, 4-6
WEEK FIVE	1 Corinthians 3:16; Hebrews 10:24-25
WEEK SIX	1 Thessalonians 5:16-18; Romans 12:1-2
WEEK SEVEN	Luke 9:23; Romans 8:28-29

Ideas for Big Steps Weekly Meetings:

Each week launches seven days of a new focus. These launching points are during your main one-on-one times with your student. They are lessons 1, 8, 15, 22, 29, 36, and 43. Lesson 50 is a Big Step also, but it is the concluding lesson preparing the lambs for their future growth and integration into their church family.

- These lessons are called "Big Steps" because they mark great accomplishments: finishing a week and starting down a new part of the trail.

- Each Big Step lesson opens with a guide to help you prepare for your meeting with your student. Your Shepherd's Guide is identical to the New Believer's Guide to make it easy to follow the journey together.

- You do not have to use these inputs, but they are there for you as prompts for insight and ideas. The top of the page will look like this:

You will want to meet face-to-face if possible for your Big Step days. You can meet virtually if you are separated geographically.

- This is an hour-long meeting where you will go through your new week's Big Step and set the stage for the next six days.

- On your first meeting with your lamb, write the day/date of your meeting on their Believer's Journey Guide.

- Always pray together.

- Ask them to say their memory verses after the first week.

- After the first week, review their lessons for questions.

- Be ahead of the weeks, so you can insert local church information as needed for lessons such as: baptism, communion, Bible studies, or ministries to be involved in.

If your student is a child, ensure that a parent is present at the weekly meetings.

Ideas for Daily Steps Encouragement:

As described in the introduction to this section, you have the privilege of ministering to your student each day through some form of contact. This does not need to be face-to-face unless you and your student already see each other daily, and this is easier for you both. This could be true for situations such as: the student is at your home, school, work, neighborhood, etc. The way you connect is up to what works best for both of you.

Contact your student in the method this is best for them.

- Phone, text, e-mail, face-to-face, Skype, etc.
- If the student is a child/minor, ensure that the parents are present and the ones receiving and passing on the messages.
- Write your contact information and theirs on the badges of page 3 in the New Believer's Guide.

Ask them how they are doing, see if they have any questions, pray with them, and let them know that you are praying for them.

Let them know that if they have questions they are free to contact you.

The Shepherd's Guide mirrors the New Believer's Guide, only your guide has lesson prompts as well as provides the answers to the questions for you.

Guidance for each week's Big Step is provided for you in the Shepherd's Guide. This gives you a lesson overview and a plan for working through this Big Step with your student.

Also provided are short prompts for each daily step so you when you contact your student. You have a quick snapshot of that day's lesson for easy reference. The top of the page looks like this:

DAILY PROMPTS FOR WEEK 1
STEPS 2-7—WHO AM I NOW?

The Big Step and prompts for the "baby steps" are given at the beginning of each week for you.

Each time you work through this material with a new student, allow the Holy Spirit to highlight something new to you. You will find He speaks to you through the lessons in a fresh way. Share your insights with your student and allow them to share their insights with you so you can grow together in faith.

Getting Ready for Week 1– Big Step 1:

As you prepare for week one, remember these things:

1. Make sure you and your lamb have coordinated the meeting details well.

   • Set the time.

   • Choose the location.

   • Make sure you have a *New Believer's Guide* to give them (if they do not already have one).

2. Do Big Step 1 in advance. Look through Steps 2-7 to know where you are headed.

3. Pray beforehand for the meeting and then together with your lamb.

4. Begin by talking and sharing your story and hearing theirs.

5. Make sure you write down the contact information for you and your student on page 3 of **50 Steps With Jesus.**

6. Walk with them through their introductory paragraphs, helping explain the purpose of *50 Steps With Jesus—New Believer's Guide,* and how their daily lessons will work.

7. The page numbers in the *Shepherd's Guide* will be different because you have additional materials included in this book. However, actual lessons (steps) mirror the *New Believer's Guide* and the layout of these pages in this book is an exact copy of actual lessons (steps) in the *New Believer's Guide.* It will be easy to follow along, you will just begin Big Steps on a different page in your guide book.

8. Each week begins with a new focus. Your *Shepherd's Guide* gives you ideas for shepherding your student and provides answers to some of the lesson's questions. Use these helps as the Holy Spirit leads you.

May the Lord richly bless you and your lamb as you meet with Him. This is exciting!

PRAYER FOCUS

Write down the focus for your prayers for your student. Perhaps they have a difficult family situation, need the strength to cut ties with some unhealthy friendships, need employment or promotion. Get to know them a little and find out what they want to lift before the Lord so you can come into agreement with them during these 50 days together.

At the end of the 50 days, show this list to your student so the two of you can rejoice over the prayers God has answered for them!

_____

_____

_____

_____

_____

_____

_____

_____

_____

_____

_____

_____

_____

_____

_____

_____

_____

_____

_____

_____

Week One

Who Am I Now?

Therefore if anyone is in Christ, he is a new creature;
the old things passed away; behold, new things have come.

2 Corinthians 5:17

SHEPHERD'S GUIDE BIG STEP 1

LESSON OVERVIEW—WHO AM I NOW?

Be excited for your student; their decision to embark on this journey is a big deal!

The theme of this week is **living the reality of their new faith.** Have them share their story with you.

The lesson opens with 2 Corinthians 2:17 and describes this new life as a beginning and a new creation.

- Go through the lesson on your own before meeting with your student. Have them answer the questions that are open-ended, then discuss them together.

- When you discuss what it means to be a new creature, help them understand that when the Lord enters your life, He creates you spiritually new and different than before. Share with them that the reason for being made "righteous" is to allow us to have a relationship with God. God desires for them to be part of His family; He saved them so they could walk with Him and experience His extravagant love.

- Psalm 1:1-6 will be a theme of the *50 Steps*. They can find this on page 13 of the New Believer's Guide. As believers, we want to be like the tree in verse 3. Throughout this guide, this truth will be reinforced—the Holy Spirit uses these three elements to help us grow:

  - prayer

  - the Word

  - the church

  You will show them how this works all through the *50 Steps*. Entire weeks are dedicated to each of the streams (prayer, the Bible, and the church).

- Introduce them to their first memory verses, Psalm 1:2-3. Introduce them to Daily Steps.

- Make sure you have their information and discuss how you will contact them.

- Remind them of how you will communicate each day.

- Ask if they have any questions?

- Pray for their growth.

Learning to Walk Daily With the Lord

Daily Prompts for Week 1
Steps 2-7—Who Am I Now?

Check in with your student each day to encourage them in their faith, to pray with them, and to develop your relationship with them. This is an important time in their life, and you are there to nurture and guide them in this journey. Following are some prompts that will help you as you connect with them each day.

Step 2—Tell Them You Are Proud of Them!

The Righteous Person
- See if they understand "assembly."
- Ask how their prayer went.
- See if they have any questions.

Step 3—Ask About How Much God Loves Them.

- 14 times or more = love/beloved
- Ask about their memory verse.

Step 4—Tell Them You Are Praying for Them.

- Ask how their prayers went.

Step 5—Remind Them They Are Righteous Because They Are in Christ.

Verb	Location	Types of People
walk	in the council	wicked
stand	path	sinners
sit	seat	scoffers

- They may ask about the "law of the Lord" or what meditation is. Both will be discussed more later, but you can fill in their questions as you feel led.

Step 6—Reinforce That They Are a New Creation.

- This is an exciting lesson where the believer ought to have something they are excited about as a new creation.

Step 7—Celebrate Completing a Full Week!

- The church is introduced in this lesson. Make sure they are being connected to the body of believers.
- Remind them of their memory verses and polish up yours.
- Prepare for Week 2 – Big Step 8.

Learning to Walk Daily With the Lord

STEP 1 — WHO AM I NOW?

Congratulations!

Being a Christian is the most wonderful thing that can ever happen to you! You are like a newly born lamb that is learning about its new world, filled with excitement.

This guide will help you take your first steps with Jesus as a new Christian. Since Jesus is with you and in you, you are not alone. You also have your shepherd to pray for you and guide you as you grow. Today, you begin to learn more about this new life!

Pray with your shepherd and then read the Bible verse from 2 Corinthians 5:17 below:

Therefore if anyone is <u>in Christ</u>, he is a new creature;
the old things passed away; behold, new things have come.

What does it mean to be "in Christ"? You are "in Christ" when you have given your life to Jesus as Lord and asked Him to forgive your sins. The Holy Spirit now lives in you. He will guide you as you learn to walk with Jesus. Your shepherd will also be there for you, listening to the Holy Spirit, and helping you along the way.

Look again at the verse above and answer the following questions:

What are the results of being in Christ? List the benefits of being a Christian below.

1. ___You are a new creature.___

2. ___The old things have passed away.___

3. ___New things have come.___

What does the first benefit you listed mean to you?

_____

_____

Say this prayer to the Lord: "Thank You, God, for making me a new creature."

What is the second benefit? Write what this benefit means to you.

_____

_____

Spend a moment to silently thank the Lord again for taking away your old life.

The third benefit of being "in Christ" is that new things have come. Wonderful new things are in store for you. As you journey with Jesus, you will discover these new things.

One of these new things is having a right relationship with God because He has taken away your sins. God forgives your sins and makes you "right" with Him. Being right with God is called being "righteous."

The following Bible verses from Psalm 1:1-6 illustrate your new life as a Christian.

PSALM 1:1-6

*¹How __blessed__ is the __man__ who does not walk in the counsel of the wicked,
nor stand in the path of sinners, nor sit in the seat of scoffers!
²But __his__ delight is in the law of the LORD, and in His law __he__ meditates
day and night. ³__He__ will be like a tree firmly planted by streams of water,
which yields its fruit in its season and its leaf does not wither;
and in whatever __he__ does, __he__ prospers.
⁴The wicked are not so, but they are like chaff
which the wind drives away. ⁵Therefore the wicked will not stand
in the judgment, nor sinners in the assembly of the __righteous__.
⁶For the LORD knows the way of the __righteous__,
but the way of the wicked will perish.*

You are now the blessed person; you are now the righteous person. Read this passage again and notice that the underlined words represent who you are now! Look through the verses again and put a circle around wicked, sinners, and scoffers.

List all the things that the blessed man is and the things he is not.

What the blessed man is:	What he is not:
Delights in God's law, meditates on it.	Walking with the wicked
Like a firmly planted tree by water	Standing with sinners
Yields fruit and doesn't wither	Sitting with scoffers
Prospers	Perishing

You want to be like the tree in verse 3. List the tree's characteristics:

1. Planted by streams of water
2. Yields its fruit in its season
3. Its leaf does not wither
4. Whatever he does, he prospers

The way a new believer grows is by getting constant nourishment from the Lord. Your shepherd will help you learn how the Holy Spirit in you nourishes you through talking with God, learning the Bible, and growing with the members of the church. Talk to God, study His Word, and fellowship with believers everyday. Just like sheep need grass and water, you as a new believer also need spiritual food and drink.

Your shepherd will prepare you for your next step and pray with you about your walk with God. Memorize Psalm 1:3 this week; let it soak in.

Write down any questions or reflections you have so you can talk about these with your shepherd.

Memorize Psalm 1:3

He will be like a tree firmly planted by streams of water, which yields its fruit in its season and its leaf does not wither; and in whatever he does, he prospers.

You can learn more about memorizing Bible verses on Step 27.

STEP 2 — GOD'S STREAMS OF WATER

Good day, child of God! Start your time with God today with this prayer—

"Thank You, God, for loving me and forgiving me.
Help me grow today as I learn more about You."

Read Psalm 1:1-6 from page 13 again.

List everything you can about the tree. Start with your list from yesterday:

1. Planted by streams of water
2. Yields its fruit in its season
3. Its leaf does not wither
4. Whatever he does, he prospers
5. The wind cannot drive it away

Who is the tree an example for? (hint: Look at verses 1-2.)

The blessed and righteous person.

Since you are now righteous in God's eyes, this is for you!

What does this person do in verse 2?

The blessed person delights in the law of the LORD

and meditates on God's law day and night.

You are looking intently into the Word and doing what a righteous person does right now.

What does this person do in verse 5?

The blessed person will stand in the judgment

in the assembly of the righteous.

Your shepherd teacher is a part of the assembly of the ones who are righteous and so are you. This assembly is your local church family and other times that you meet with believers who are part of God's family from other churches.

How to pray:

Prayer is as simple as talking to God, just like you would speak with a friend.

It doesn't have to be formal; there are no specific words you have to say, just talk to Him about what is on your mind or in your heart.

Start with the prayer at the beginning of Step 2, and then just say whatever comes to mind. You can tell God anything! He always loves hearing from you.

As you grow in your walk with Jesus, you will focus on these three streams for help. They are: talking with God, reading His Word, and being a part of His church family.

Ask your shepherd any questions you have and share with your shepherd insights the Lord has given you about your new life with Him.

Finish your time with the Lord praying your memory verse from Psalms 1:3. Pray this as a promise applied to your life.

"Dear Lord, I want to be like a tree firmly planted by streams of water, which yields its fruit in its season, and its leaf does not wither. In whatever I do, help me prosper. In Your name, Jesus, I pray. Amen."

Step 3 — GOD LOVES YOU

Can it be any more wonderful than this—God loves you! Slowly thank Him again for loving you.

"Thank you God for loving me … for loving me … for loving me. I love You, God … I love You, God … I love You, God … I love You!"

As you read these verses from God's Word, see God's love shine through them. **Circle love and beloved:**

See how great a love the Father has bestowed on us, that we would be called children of God; and such we are.

1 JOHN 3:1

⁷Beloved, let us love one another, for love is from God; and everyone who loves is born of God and knows God. ⁸The one who does not love does not know God, for God is love. ⁹By this the love of God was manifested in us, that God sent His only begotten Son into the world so that we might live through Him. ¹⁰In this is love, not that we loved God, but that He loved us and sent His Son to be the propitiation (price) for our sins. ¹¹Beloved, if God so loved us, we also ought to love one another.

1 JOHN 4:7-11

50 STEPS WITH JESUS

Learning to Walk Daily With the Lord

We ⟨love⟩ because He first ⟨loved⟩ us.
1 JOHN 4:19

Do you feel loved by God, or is it a struggle to believe this?

His love for you is because of HIS goodness; it isn't because of anything you could ever do to earn it or deserve it. He loves you because you are His child. He loves you because He is love.

You are extravagantly loved by God.

Now count your circled words. How many times did you circle love and beloved? __16__

God really loves us, and so we really love Him!

God went to great effort and expense to bring you into the family. None of us earns it or deserves it. It is a gift motivated by God's love for you and His desire to journey through this life with you!

Pray:

> *"Dear Lord, I want to thank You again for loving me and making me Your child. Help me to know You more each day. Help me to love like You love. In Your name, Jesus, I pray. Amen."*

Write your questions or what you learned to share with your shepherd:

_____

_____

_____

_____

_____

_____

_____

———— ◆———◇———◆ ————

STEP 4 — GOD WANTS YOU TO TALK WITH HIM

Good news for you today—the Creator of the universe wants to speak with you! Ask Him how He is doing.

> *"Good day, God. I love You. Thank You, God, for wanting to talk with me. Help me to listen to You all of the time and talk with You with both my thoughts and my voice."*

Prayer is one of the three great streams of water where the tree is planted and finds life in Psalm 1 (in Step 1 of your guide). Christians pray all the time. You can pray with others or by yourself, with your eyes opened or closed, as a song or a poem, or just by what you are saying or thinking. Some people find it helpful to write their prayers. What makes it a prayer is that you are saying or thinking it to God. You are communicating with God. God created you to do this with Him.

In fact, early in the Bible when Adam was in the garden, he talked with God every day. When Adam and Eve sinned, that relationship changed. On Step One, you studied this verse:

Therefore if anyone is in Christ, he is a new creature;
the old things passed away; behold, new things have come.

2 CORINTHIANS 5:17

Because Jesus forgave your sins, one of the new things you have is the privilege to pray with God as one of His children. This is even better than Adam and Eve had. With the Holy Spirit in you, you can talk to God all the time!

Here are three great verses for you as you think about your new life as a believer.

[16]Rejoice always; [17]pray without ceasing; [18]in everything give thanks;
for this is God's will for you in Christ Jesus.

1 THESSALONIANS 5:16-18

This is going to be a great journey. Your heavenly tour guide wants you to be able to go through this life with joy, talking constantly with Him, and being thankful for all things. Pray this prayer:

"God, help me to be joyful always, to pray without ceasing, and to be
thankful in all circumstances! I look forward to talking with You!
Help me to listen as well."

Keep working on your memory verse Psalm 1:3. Tomorrow you will add Psalm 1:2.

But his delight is in the law of the LORD,
and in His law he meditates day and night.

PSALM 1:2

He will be like a tree firmly planted by streams of water,
which yields its fruit in its season and its leaf does not wither;
and in whatever he does, he prospers.

PSALM 1:3

Tips to memorize:

Write the verse you wish to memorize on a note card and tape it to your mirror; put it on your refrigerator or the visor of your car.

Read the verse out loud several times each day.

Sing the verse—you may find that putting it to music helps you remember the words!

Write your questions or what you learned to share with your shepherd:

_____

_____

_____

_____

_____

_____

_____

STEP 5 — GOD WANTS YOU TO KNOW HIS WORD

Happy days ... guess what? More good news! The Creator of the universe has given you a love letter. It is the Bible!

Spend some time thanking God on your own for His love, for prayer, and for the Bible. Finish with:

The Bible is God's love letter to you!

> *"Lord, help me to love Your Word, to study it, and hear You speak to me through it. In Your name, Jesus, I pray. Amen."*

The Bible is another stream that the Holy Spirit uses in your life to make you like the tree that does not wither and that bears fruit in season. Look at the printed page of Psalm 1 on page 13 again. Draw a square around the verbs of verse 1 that describe what the blessed man is not doing. List what the blessed man is not doing on the chart below:

How blessed is the man who does not:

Verb	Location	Types of People
walk	counsel	wicked
stand	path	sinners
sit	seat	scoffers

Rather than be interested in, invest time in, or be influenced by the wicked, sinners, and scoffers, this person has found the true source of knowledge.

Now notice the traits of the righteous man in your new memory verse, Psalm 1:2.

But his delight is in the law of the LORD,
and in His law he meditates day and night.

Where is his delight? ___The law of the Lord___.

How often does he meditate on the Lord's law? ___day___ and ___night___.

As you walk with the Lord, you will grow in your understanding of the Bible. You will learn more about how to read it. In two and a half weeks, you will spend an entire week learning about the Bible and how to study it better. For now, keep memorizing your verses, doing your lessons, and reading the Bible on your own if you want to do so. Your shepherd can help you with this.

Keep working on your memory verses: Psalm 1:2 and 3. Talk to God as you memorize. Ask Him to help you remember His words.

Write your questions or what you learned to share with your shepherd.

_____

_____

_____

_____

_____

_____

STEP 6 — GOD MADE YOU A NEW CREATION

Just a reminder—You are a new creation. Today you will learn a little more about what you learned on day one.

Therefore if anyone is in Christ, <u>he is a new creature;</u>
the old things passed away; behold, new things have come.
2 CORINTHIANS 5:17

You are a new creature—a new creation!

When you gave your heart to God, you became a new creation as you were united with Christ by faith. As He entered your spirit, you were regenerated. What was dead because it was separated from God is now made alive through union with Him—a brand new creature, a brand new creation!

Memorize Psalm 1:2-3

²But his delight is in the law of the LORD, and in His law he meditates day and night.

³He will be like a tree firmly planted by streams of water, which yields its fruit in its season and its leaf does not wither; and in whatever he does, he prospers.

Pray this prayer:

"Lord, help me understand what it means to be a new creation."

Review your notes from day 1. Does this all make sense to you?

Read the Bible verse from 2 Corinthians 5:17 again:

Therefore if anyone is in Christ, he is a new creature; the old things passed away; behold, new things have come.

This word for creature is used to describe a new kind of life that had not happened before Jesus went to heaven. It describes you as a different being. In James 1:18, it is described this way:

In the exercise of His will He brought us forth by the word of truth so that we would be a kind of first fruits among His creatures.

There were no Christians prior to the time Jesus ascended into heaven and sent the Holy Spirit to live in believers. When you realize your need for salvation, repent, believe, and seek Jesus as the Savior and surrender to Him as Lord (Romans 10:9-10, 13), you are "born again" into a new being, one that was not available until after Jesus lived, died, rose again, and ascended to heaven.

You are changed to be this new creature with the spiritual DNA and bloodline of the children of God! Wow! There was a man who came to talk with Jesus about how to enter the Kingdom of God. Jesus said, "You must be born again." He did not understand how. Jesus indicated that this birth was spiritual and was by faith (John 3:1-21).

As you read this, you may have one of two reactions. The first reaction is being joyful that God has recreated your spirit within and made you His child. You know you are the recipient of a miraculous act of love and forgiveness in response to your surrender and faith. You are very aware of the Lord in your life.

The second reaction might be uncertainty that you have truly encountered and been changed by Jesus in your life. If so, this may be the most important day in your life. Regardless of how good or religious or knowledgeable you may be, you need to be sure that you truly are a recreated, born-again, follower of Jesus. Speak with your shepherd about this and find peace on this issue. If you do not already have this relationship with Jesus, then today may be the true day of your salvation!

Now pray, *"Lord, thank You for loving me so much that You recreated me so that I could be with You forever. Help me to walk this new life with You."*

Keep working on your memory verses Psalm 1:2 and 3.

Write your questions or what you learned to share with your shepherd.

_____

_____

_____

_____

_____

_____

STEP 7— GOD MADE YOU PART OF HIS FAMILY

You have now had one week of walking with Jesus ... how exciting!

Pray this prayer:

> *"Lord, help me understand what it means to be in a new family.*
> *Thank You that I am not walking with You all alone;*
> *I belong to a family—Your family!"*

You belong to a family … God's family!

Being a part of the family of God is very important for your growth as a believer. Along with prayer and the Word of God, it is one of the three main streams that the Holy Spirit uses to help you grow. There will be an entire week dedicated to being a part of the Christian family. During that week, you will see how much the Holy Spirit is doing to help the family grow.

The church is described as a body or a family or even an assembly. Look at verses 4-6 of Psalm 1, printed below.

Put a box around the words "wicked" and "sinners." Underline the consequences of those who are not in God's favor:

> ⁴*The* wicked *are not so, but they are like chaff which the wind drives away.* ⁵*Therefore the* wicked *will not stand in the judgment, nor* sinners *in the assembly of the righteous.* ⁶*For the LORD knows the way of the righteous, but the way of the* wicked *will perish.*

List what you discovered about the wicked and sinners:

They are like chaff the wind drives away

They will not stand in the judgment

In Jesus' name I pray. Amen."

They will not be in the assembly of the righteous

They wiill perish

Based on these verses, what do you learn about the righteous?

They will not be driven away

They will stand in the judgment

They will be in the congregation of the righteous

The Lord knows (this word means "intimately knows" in Hebrew, the language of the Old Testament) the way of the righteous

They will not perish

As a child of God, you are a part of the assembly of the righteous. You have a permanent, imperishable status. You will not meet the same judgment as the wicked. God's family, like your shepherd, is invested in helping you walk in the way of the righteous, for this is your way now.

How do you feel about joining a church family? Are you excited about this or do you have some reservations? Write these below and ask your shepherd questions you have about being a part of the church.

Polish your two memory verses from Psalm 1:2-3.

Pray:

"Lord, thank You for this great week of learning about Your love for me, how to pray, and how important the Word and the church are to help me grow strong in my relationship with You. Help me grow each day closer to You. Thank You for my shepherd, _____.
In Jesus' name I pray. Amen."

Memorize Psalm 1:2-3

²But his delight is in the law of the LORD, and in His law he meditates day and night.

³He will be like a tree firmly planted by streams of water, which yields its fruit in its season and its leaf does not wither; and in whatever he does, he prospers.

Week Two

Following Jesus

... having been buried with Him in baptism, in which you were also raised up with Him through faith in the working of God, who raised Him from the dead.

Colossians 2:12

SHEPHERD'S GUIDE
BIG STEP 8

LESSON OVERVIEW—FOLLOWING JESUS BY WALKING WITH HIM

The theme of this week is **following Jesus**. Some may be troubled by the ideas of Lordship and obedience, but they are routine parts of the Christian life. As believers, it is important that they learn to faithfully follow Jesus by trusting Him. The Holy Spirit will help them do this, and as they do, they will be more like Jesus and know Him better.

Begin your time with prayer, answer any questions, ask them to recite their memory verses to you.

As they describe what they noticed about being a new creation, celebrate these changes with them. If they appear to have no awareness of change or no understanding of Christ in them, have them share their faith story with you to reassure them regarding their salvation.

- The crosses and hearts are indicated in your lesson guide along with answers.

- They have learned about these promises after obedience:

    - Father will love

    - Jesus will love

    - Jesus will reveal/disclose/manifest Himself to the one who is obedient because of love

- Ask your student these questions:

    - Since God already loves you, what do you think this means?

    - Disclose means to show or reveal. Therefore, as you walk in greater obedience, you will get to know Jesus even more. What do you think about this?

    - Is there anything that the Lord is asking you to do that you need to do but have not yet done?

    - Do you have any questions?

- Introduce them to their memory verses: John 14:15 and 21.

- Share with your student any concluding thoughts you have.

- Give them an overview of Steps 9-15. Each of these days has a different way to follow Jesus. If your church has anything more specific for communion or baptism, this is a great time to introduce this.

- Pray with your student and continue to encourage them.

Learning to Walk Daily With the Lord

DAILY PROMPTS FOR WEEK 2
STEPS 9-14—FOLLOWING JESUS

Check in with your student each day to encourage them, to pray with them, and to continue developing your relationship with them. Here are some prompts that will help you as you connect with them each day.

STEP 9—TELL THEM YOU ARE PROUD OF THEM!

- Ask them about the lesson and baptism. If they are not already baptized, encourage them to take this important step. See if they have questions or need to speak with a staff member at your church.

STEP 10—ENCOURAGE THEM IN FOLLOWING JESUS.

- Ask about their memory verse and about any questions regarding baptism or communion.

STEP 11—TELL THEM YOU ARE PRAYING FOR THEM.

- Ask who they thought of to share with. Ask them how they will meet with them to share.

STEP 12—PRAY FOR THEM.

- Ask if they have any questions about loving others or if they are struggling with this.

STEP 13—BE SENSITIVE AS ISSUES WITH UNFORGIVENESS MAY ARISE.

- The Holy Spirit is at work in your student. Studying about forgiveness can bring things to the surface that will need to be brought into the light and surrendered to the Father. Remind them of God's great love and how He has forgiven us of so much. It is His power which enables us to walk in forgiveness, even when the one who has wronged us is unrepentant. Perhaps your student is realizing they have some areas where they have hurt others and need to ask for forgiveness as well.

- When you complete Step 15, you may need to revisit this subject together.

STEP 14—CELEBRATE COMPLETING TWO WEEKS!

- Ask about their lesson on Service and encourage them in their progress as they get ready to begin Week 3.

- Prepare for Week 3 – Big Step 15.

STEP 8—FOLLOWING JESUS BY WALKING WITH HIM

Congratulations—you have completed week one!

You learned how much Jesus loves you and that He desires a relationship with you.

It just gets better from here …

Following Jesus doesn't mean that you are walking behind Him. Jesus is walking with you every moment of the day and every step of the way, teaching you what it means to be in a relationship with Him.

As you start this time with your shepherd, begin with prayer and thank the Lord for saving you and making you one of His children.

This week you get to learn about a very important principle of following Jesus. The principle is **trust** or obedience. Today you will learn why it is important to God that you trust Him and why it is important to you for your growth. You will also learn this week about the importance of following Jesus in your relationships with other people. Today you start with a term called "Lordship."

Read the Bible verse from Romans 10:9-10 and 13 below:

> *⁹If you confess with your mouth Jesus as Lord, and believe in your heart that God raised Him from the dead, you will be saved; ¹⁰for with the heart a person believes, resulting in righteousness, and with the mouth he confesses, resulting in salvation. ¹³For "WHOEVER WILL CALL ON THE NAME OF THE LORD WILL BE SAVED."*

Lordship rules! Lordship is a term that many do not understand right away since it is not used as much as it once was. The word can sometimes mean boss or owner. In some countries, it is a title of a landowner. In the time of Jesus, the term "Lord" had a huge meaning. It meant supreme ruler or god. The Romans required every person to declare every year that "Caesar is Lord." In this act, the subjects vowed their greatest allegiance in life to their ruler, Caesar. The Christians would not do it since "Jesus is Lord!"

Mark with a cross the words "Jesus," "Lord," and "Him" in Romans 10:9-10 and 13.

From what you marked, what do you discover about what Jesus does for you as a result of being your Lord?

1. Jesus saves you.

2. Jesus gives you His righteousness.

3. Jesus gives you salvation.

TRUST (n):

firm belief in the reliability, truth, ability, or strength of someone or something

Shepherd's Note:

In Greek, the language of the New Testament, "save" is the word *sozo* and it means "to rescue from danger or destruction, to save from perishing." In Psalm 1:6, "the way of the wicked will perish," but the righteous will not perish because they have called on the name of the LORD to save them.

In Romans 10:13, the term "Lord" is taken from a book in the Bible called Joel. Joel was written hundreds of years before Jesus was born, yet contains a quote about Him. Read Joel 2:32:

> "And it will come about that whoever calls on the name of the LORD will be delivered; for on Mount Zion and in Jerusalem there will be those who escape, as the LORD has said, even among the survivors whom the LORD calls."

This is one of the many verses that helps you understand that Jesus is both man and God.

Lordship is very important in your Christian walk. It means that you make Jesus the ruler or boss of your life. You give Him control. You desire to do His will for your life over your own will. It is amazing what God will do in your life if you let Him lead you throughout your life.

Look at these next two verses, John 14:15 and 21. Start memorizing them as your verses for this week.

"If you love Me, you will keep My commandments."
JOHN 14:15

"He who has My commandments and keeps them is the one who loves Me; and he who loves Me will be loved by My Father, and I will love him and will disclose Myself to him."
JOHN 14:21

Put a heart on the word "love." How many hearts are there? _____5_____

Look at John 14:15 and 21 again; mark the pronouns for Jesus with a cross.

What motivates obedience in the first phrase?

_____
Loving Jesus motivates you to keep His commandments.
_____

Commandments in these verses are much broader than the Ten Commandments and the Law. This is anything that Jesus tells you to do. You will hear the Lord lead you through many ways. You can hear the Lord in the three streams of your study of the Bible, your prayer life, and your church life. There are other ways as well since God is great at communicating. More later!

Memorize John 14:15, 21

15If you love Me, you will keep My commandments.

21He who has My commandments and keeps them is the one who loves Me; and he who loves Me will be loved by My Father, and I will love him and will disclose Myself to him.

In your memory verse, John 14:21, what promises are there for you after you obey?

1.   You will be loved by the Father.

2.   Jesus will love you.

3.   Jesus will disclose Himself to you.

Since God already loves you, what do you think this means?

This love between you, Jesus, and God the Father is a deep, rich, intimate love because of your saving relationship with Jesus Christ. God loves you and wants you to know Him because you are in a relationship with Him.

Disclose means to show or reveal. Therefore, once you obey, you will get to know Jesus even more.

Is there anything that the Lord is asking you to do that you need to do but have not yet?

_____

_____

_____

_____

_____

Write down any thoughts or questions to review with your shepherd.

_____

_____

_____

_____

_____

Pray to close:

"You are Lord of my life, Jesus. You are Lord of the universe.
I want You to lead my life. I want to love You and follow Your
commands. Help me to be lovingly obedient."

STEP 9—FOLLOWING JESUS BY BEING BAPTIZED

Begin by thanking God for this day. Today is exciting as you begin looking at ways the Lord wants you to follow Him. Your shepherd will be very important in helping you understand baptism and communion. A couple of things to know about baptism: 1) It is a big deal to the Lord. Jesus was baptized, and He told us to be baptized as a testimony of being Christian. 2) Baptism is seen by most of the world as the single greatest act identifying you as a follower of Jesus.

Read Acts 8:26-39.

26But an angel of the Lord spoke to Philip saying, "Get up and go south to the road that descends from Jerusalem to Gaza." (This is a desert road.) 27So he got up and went; and there was an Ethiopian eunuch, a court official of Candace, queen of the Ethiopians, who was in charge of all her treasure; and he had come to Jerusalem to worship, 28and he was returning and sitting in his chariot, and was reading the prophet Isaiah.

29Then the Spirit said to Philip, "Go up and join this chariot."

30Philip ran up and heard him reading Isaiah the prophet, and said, "Do you understand what you are reading?"

31And he said, "Well, how could I, unless someone guides me?"

And he invited Philip to come up and sit with him. 32Now the passage of Scripture which he was reading was this: "HE WAS LED AS A SHEEP TO SLAUGHTER; AND AS A LAMB BEFORE ITS SHEARER IS SILENT, SO HE DOES NOT OPEN HIS MOUTH. 33"IN HUMILIATION HIS JUDGMENT WAS TAKEN AWAY; WHO WILL RELATE HIS GENERATION? FOR HIS LIFE IS REMOVED FROM THE EARTH."

34The eunuch answered Philip and said, "Please tell me, of whom does the prophet say this? Of himself or of someone else?"

35Then Philip opened his mouth, and beginning from this Scripture he preached Jesus to him. 36As they went along the road they came to some water; and the eunuch *said, "Look! Water! What prevents me from being baptized?"

37And Philip said, "If you believe with all your heart, you may."

Baptism is an important sign of your new relationship with God.

Following Jesus by being baptized identifies you as a child of God!

50 STEPS WITH JESUS   43

And he answered and said, "I believe that Jesus Christ is the Son of God." [38] And he ordered the chariot to stop; and they both went down into the water, Philip as well as the eunuch, and he baptized him. [39] When they came up out of the water, the Spirit of the Lord snatched Philip away; and the eunuch no longer saw him, but went on his way rejoicing.

Was the man excited about following Jesus? How do you know?

YES! He said he believed Jesus Christ is the Son of God, and he wanted to be baptized.

What did he want to do? What was required for baptism?

He wanted to be baptized. In order to be baptized, he had to confess that Jesus Christ is the Son of God, and he had to go down into the water.

If you have not been baptized yet, ask your shepherd to help you be obedient to the Lord in this very important display of your faith.

Pray:

*"Thank You, God, for loving me and forgiving me.
Help me be faithful to what You ask me to do."*

———— ◆—◇—◆ ————

STEP 10—FOLLOWING JESUS BY CELEBRATING COMMUNION

Today is exciting because you get to see another part of Jesus' love for you. In the church this is called communion. Thank Him again for dying for you!

*"Thank You, God, for loving me … for dying for me … for living for me.
I love You, God! Help me understand how important
communion is to You and the church."*

Memorize John 14:15, 21

[15] If you love Me, you will keep My commandments.

[21] He who has My commandments and keeps them is the one who loves Me; and he who loves Me will be loved by My Father, and I will love him and will disclose Myself to him.

Read Matthew 26:26-29.

26While they were eating, Jesus took some bread, and after a blessing, He broke it and gave it to the disciples, and said, "Take, eat; this is My body." 27And when He had taken a cup and given thanks, He gave it to them, saying, "Drink from it, all of you; 28for this is My blood of the covenant, which is poured out for many for forgiveness of sins. 29But I say to you, I will not drink of this fruit of the vine from now on until that day when I drink it new with you in My Father's kingdom."

Mark the words "Jesus," "I," "He," and "My" with a cross. List what Jesus did:

1) Jesus took some bread and said a blessing.   2) He broke the bread and gave it to His disciples.   3) He told them to eat the bread because it is His body.   4) He took a cup and gave thanks.

5) He gave it to His disciples and told them to drink because it is His blood of the covenant poured out for the forgiveness of the sins.

Underline the word "you." How many did you underline? _____3_____

Who is the "you" in this passage? _____Jesus' disciples_____

As a Christian, this applies to you as well. Also, you will get to be with Jesus when He observes this celebration again!

Communion is important because it is a vivid reminder of what Jesus did for us as our sacrifice on the cross. His human, sinless body was offered as a sacrifice for our sins. His blood was poured out to cover our sins. Hebrews 9:22 says, "*...without shedding of blood there is no forgiveness.*"

As you grow, you will learn more about the Jewish ceremonies like Passover and the sacrificial system that God instituted to help purify the people. But, regardless of how much you understand these things now, you are greatly benefited by the perfect sacrifice of the man named Jesus who died for you.

Communion is the celebration of Jesus's life, death, and resurrection. We do this in remembrance of Him.

Pray:

"Dear Lord, I want to thank You again for loving me and forgiving me. Help me to celebrate communion with deep appreciation for You and Your gift of life to me. In Your name, Jesus, I pray. Amen."

Communion is the celebration of the life, death, and resurrection of Jesus. Participating in communion helps us remember what He did for us and compels us to worship.

Write your questions or what you learned to share with your shepherd:

_____

_____

_____

_____

_____

_____

_____

☑ Baptism

☑ Communion

☑ Tell Others

STEP 11—FOLLOWING JESUS BY SHARING YOUR STORY

Good day to you, new believer! Today is the third act of trust for you as a Christian. Baptism and communion are actions that tell others you are a follower of Jesus, a Christian. Pray that in this lesson God will show you someone to share your Christian story with.

Pray:

"Good day, God. Thank You, for saving me and changing my life. Lead me to someone so I can tell them about what You have done in my life."

Just as the Lord wants us to be baptized and take communion, He also wants us to tell others that we are Christians. He is very serious about telling others that we are Christians. Here are Jesus' thoughts on this.

³²"Therefore everyone who confesses Me before men, I will also confess him before My Father who is in heaven. ³³But whoever denies Me before men, I will also deny him before My Father who is in heaven."

MATTHEW 10:32-33

Mark the pronouns used for Jesus ("Me," "I," and "My") with a cross. What do you think Jesus means in these verses?

When you acknowledge that you belong to Jesus in front of others, Jesus acknowledges that you belong to Him before God the Father. If you deny that you belong to Christ, He will deny that you belong to Him before His Father.

In your study of the Bible, you will often find this kind of statement: "If this happens, then this will happen." Jesus is very clear here about how important it is to be identified with Him. He made you, died for you, gave you new life as His brother or sister, and gave you eternal life with Him. You have the family name now. Loyalty is important to God.

How many people have you told that you are now a Christian? _____

This is a type of confession or profession of your faith. This is how most Christians fulfill this act of obedience. We openly tell people that we are Christians.

For some, this confession is part of persecution. Every day around the world, believers face this kind of threat: "Denounce Jesus or die." Or maybe in a safer country it is, "You aren't really a Christian are you?"

This is a difficult challenge for some of you. God knows your circumstances and will help you be able to let others know you are a believer.

Who can you tell that you are now a Christian? Write their names below.

_____

_____

_____

_____

Continue memorizing John 14:15 and 21.

Pray:

"Lord, help me to share my faith openly with _____ and _____. Give me strength and help me not to fail to tell others about You."

Memorize John 14:15, 21

[15]If you love Me, you will keep My commandments.

[21]He who has My commandments and keeps them is the one who loves Me; and he who loves Me will be loved by My Father, and I will love him and will disclose Myself to him.

STEP 12—FOLLOWING JESUS BY LOVING OTHERS

Happy days! Guess what? There is more good news about God's love and your ability to love as a result of Him being in you. You have looked at three important ways of showing you're a believer: baptism, communion, and telling others that you are a Christian. Now you will learn three acts of obedience that are behaviors of Jesus being expressed through us.

Spend some time asking God to help you love others:

"Lord, help me to love Your people with all of my heart, just like You do, Lord. In Your name, Jesus, I pray, Amen."

On Step 3, you circled "love" and "beloved" in verses from 1 John. The word for love is a special word that means a love like God's love. It is unselfish and unending. **This time underline the phrases that talk about you loving others.**

See how great a love the Father has bestowed on us, that we would be called children of God; and such we are.

1 JOHN 3:1

⁷Beloved, <u>let us love one another,</u> for love is from God; and <u>everyone who loves is born of God and knows God</u>. ⁸The one who does not love does not know God, for God is love. ⁹By this the love of God was manifested in us, that God sent His only begotten Son into the world so that we might live through Him. ¹⁰In this is love, not that we loved God, but that He loved us and sent His Son to be the price for our sins. ¹¹Beloved, <u>if God so loved us, we also ought to love one another.</u>

1 JOHN 4:7-11

<u>We love because He first loved us.</u>

1 JOHN 4:19

How many phrases did you find? 4

Which one is most special to you?

_____

_____

_____

What are some ways you can love unselfishly?

_____

_____

_____

_____

Keep working on your memory verses. Write John 14:15 and 21 in the space below.

_____

_____

_____

_____

_____

_____

Write your questions or what you learned to share with your shepherd:

_____

_____

_____

_____

_____

_____

_____

STEP 13—FOLLOWING JESUS BY FORGIVING OTHERS

Dear new creation, "all things become new." Today you will learn about one of the most powerful behaviors of Christians. It is forgiveness.

Pray:

"Lord, help me understand as a new creation how I can forgive and who I should forgive. Amen."

> "To be a Christian means to forgive the inexcusable because God has forgiven the inexcusable in you."
>
> —C.S. Lewis

Forgiveness is a behavior of God. It is the removal of a debt owed to God from our behavior of sin. Sins are things we think, say, or do that are wrong. Sins are also things we do not do that we should. We all sin. We all fall short of God's standard of holiness. But God wants a relationship with us, so He makes a way for us to be forgiven. Jesus is the way. When we believe that Jesus died for our sins and we ask in faith for God to forgive us, He does. Read this wonderful promise!

If we confess our sins, He is faithful and righteous to forgive us our sins and to cleanse us from all unrighteousness.

I JOHN 1:9

What are God's virtues that form the foundation of the promises in this verse?

God is faithful.

God is righteous.

What does God do for us when we confess our sin?

When we confess our sins: God forgives our sins.

God cleanses all our unrighteousness.

Forgiveness, like love, is an act of obedience for Christians.

14For if you forgive others for their transgressions, your heavenly Father will also forgive you. 15But if you do not forgive others, then your Father will not forgive your transgressions.

MATTHEW 6:14-15

Understanding this principle helps us practice forgiveness and accept God's forgiveness. A good definition of forgiveness is **to release someone from a real or perceived debt or wrong that they owe you.** Jesus, in Mark 11, teaches us about the urgency for forgiving and the effects of unforgiveness on our own relationship with God.

Whenever you stand praying, forgive, if you have anything against anyone, so that your Father who is in heaven will also forgive you your transgressions.

MARK 11:25

Is there someone in your life that you need to forgive? Ask God to help you forgive them.

Pray:

"Lord, thank You for loving me so much that You forgave me. Help me to forgive _____."

Keep working on your memory verses from John 14:15 and 21.

STEP 14—FOLLOWING JESUS BY SERVING OTHERS

Congratulations! Step 14. Two weeks of walking with Jesus! This week you have focused on baptism, communion, telling others about Jesus, loving others like Jesus, and forgiveness. Today we will talk about what it means to serve others the way Jesus does.

Pray:

"Lord, help me be like You and be a servant."

Just like being obedient in loving and forgiving, we are also called to be obedient in serving. The following is a very special passage of Scripture from Jesus, at His last supper with His disciples, the night before He was crucified.

Memorize John 14:15, 21

15If you love Me, you will keep My commandments.

21He who has My commandments and keeps them is the one who loves Me; and he who loves Me will be loved by My Father, and I will love him and will disclose Myself to him.

Washing the feet of guests was a very common custom in Bible times. People wore sandals, and the roads were usually dusty. The person who was tasked with washing the feet of others was the lowest slave or youngest child.

⁵Then He poured water into the basin, and began to wash the disciples' feet and to wipe them with the towel with which He was girded. ⁶So He came to Simon Peter. He said to Him, "Lord, do You wash my feet?"

⁷Jesus answered and said to him, "What I do you do not realize now, but you will understand hereafter."

⁸Peter said to Him, "Never shall You wash my feet!"

Jesus answered him, "If I do not wash you, you have no part with Me."

⁹Simon Peter said to Him, "Lord, then wash not only my feet, but also my hands and my head."

¹⁰Jesus said to him, "He who has bathed needs only to wash his feet, but is completely clean; and you are clean, but not all of you." ¹¹For He knew the one who was betraying Him; for this reason He said, "Not all of you are clean."

¹²So when He had washed their feet, and taken His garments and reclined at the table again, He said to them, "Do you know what I have done to you? ¹³You call Me Teacher and Lord; and you are right, for so I am. ¹⁴If I then, the Lord and the Teacher, washed your feet, you also ought to wash one another's feet. ¹⁵For I gave you an example that you also should do as I did to you."

JOHN 13:5-15

Who washed the feet of the disciples? _Jesus_

Who tried to stop Him from doing it? _Peter_

What two titles does Jesus refer to Himself as:

Teacher and _Lord_

Which one was studied on Step 8? (See page 40.) _Lord_

As you walk with Jesus, you will become a servant of others. In Philippians 2:3-4, we are to:

³Do nothing from selfishness or empty conceit, but with humility of mind regard one another as more important than yourselves;

Learning to Walk Daily With the Lord

*⁴do not merely look out for your own personal interests,
but also for the interests of others.*

Pray:

*"Lord, thank You for this great week with You. Help me grow closer to
You every day. Thank you for my shepherd, _____,
who is following Jesus and serving me.
In Jesus name I pray, Amen."*

Write John 14:15 and 21 out below as a memorizing tool.

_____

_____

_____

_____

_____

_____

_____

Who do you know that
you can serve like Jesus
serves?

_____

SUMMARY

From Week 1 you have learned:

- **Step 1**—Because you are in Christ, you are now a new creation.

- **Step 2**—The three streams to help you grow in your walk with the Lord are: talking with God, reading His Word, and being a part of His church family.

- **Step 3**—God loves you from His goodness; there is nothing you can ever do to earn God's love and nothing you could ever do that would make Him cease loving you. God loves you with an everlasting love.

- **Step 4**—God loves talking with you. Prayer is simply talking with God and listening for Him to speak with you.

- **Step 5**—God gave you His Word through the Bible. Meditating on His Word will strengthen you, build you, and increase your faith as you mature in Him.

- **Step 6**—You are a born-again child of God, an heir of God and a joint heir with Jesus (Romans 8:17).

- **Step 7**—You are part of God's family. Connecting meaningfully with a local church will help you learn to walk in the way of righteousness.

From Week 2 you have learned:

- **Step 8**—Jesus is not only your Savior, but also your Lord. You demonstrate your trust in Him through obedience to Him and His Word.

- **Step 9**—Baptism is an important sign of your new relationship with God. Being obedient to Jesus by being baptized pleases Him and identifies you as His follower.

- **Step 10**—Communion is the celebration of the life, death, and resurrection of Jesus. Taking it often helps you remember and celebrate what He did for you.

- **Step 11**—Telling others about Jesus, sharing your story, is an identification with Jesus and a profession of faith.

- **Step 12**—When we are filled with the love of Jesus, it is natural to begin to love others.

- **Step 13**—Because Jesus has forgiven us so incredibly, we can walk in forgiveness towards others. This forgiveness allows us to live in matchless freedom!

- **Step 14**—Serving others is a privilege and a joy when you walk with God. As Servant of All, He fills your heart with delight every time you serve others.

Learning to Walk Daily With the Lord

WEEK THREE

MORE WAYS TO TALK WITH GOD

Rejoice always; pray without ceasing; in everything give thanks;
for this is God's will for you in Christ Jesus.

1 THESSALONIANS 5:16-18

LESSON OVERVIEW—MORE WAYS TO TALK WITH GOD

The theme of this week is **prayer**. This will be the first of three weeks that focus entirely on the "Streams of Water" introduced in Psalm 1:2-3.

Ask your student if they will pray out loud with you the written prayer. If you sense that they are not comfortable even reading it out loud as a prayer, then wait. If they will, then this will be a landmark moment for them.

Show them how to mark God and pronouns for God with a triangle. The marking of the Bible verses from the beginning is to develop good study habits and make intentional observations about the richness of God's Word. Later on this will be taught in greater detail.

This is a straightforward lesson with the great goal of this week being talking with Jesus. They get to talk to the Creator of the universe. As you share, this will become normal for them. Some people have never talked with God. Your student won't be on that list!

- Help them sense the awe of talking to God. It is a marevelous privilege and blessing to the believer.

- If you have any personal reflections about the Lord's Prayer or regarding your prayer life, tell them about it. This is a great opportunity for you to share your prayer journey with the Lord.

- Their memory verses will be Matthew 6:9-13. (An optional verse is 1 John 1:9.)

- Have them share their memory verses from Week Two—John 14:15 and 21.

- Have them share their memory verses from Week One—Psalm 1:2-3.

- Answer any questions and allow them the opportunity to just talk with you.

- Provide a brief overview of Steps 16-21. Each of these days has a different way to pray to God.

- Close in prayer.

Daily Prompts for Week 3
Steps 16-21—More Ways to Talk With God

Check in with your student each day to encourage them, to pray with them, and to continue developing your relationship with them. Here are some prompts that will help you as you connect with them each day.

Step 16—Tell Them You Are Proud of How Much They Have Learned.

- Thanksgiving is such a powerful prayer. Ask them if they were able to trust the Lord with issues.

- Pray for them to really desire to talk to the LORD, to understand what a precious gift from God prayer is.

Step 17—Talk With Them About Praise.

- Ask them what was special about praise.

- Share with them your own experience with praising God.

Step 18—Encourage Them.

- Confession can be difficult since we discover things in our lives as we grow. Remind your student that the Lord is the one who is faithful to forgive (1 John 1:9). We often have to confess something every day, but once it is confessed, we need to trust God to forgive us. Satan wants us to feel guilty about the things for which we have already been forgiven.

- They may have deep things within that God wants them to know that His forgiveness is greater than. Remind them that there is now no condemnation for those in Christ Jesus (Romans 8:1). The Holy Spirit convicts us of sin not to bring us shame, but to allow us the joy that comes through confession (James 4:7-10) and being in right standing with God.

Step 19—Pray for Them.

- Encourage them and ask if there is a petition that you could help them pray for.

Step 20—Encourage Them to Continue Speaking With God Daily.

- Ask about their list and if there is someone specific on their list that you can pray in agreement for with them. Help them find Scripture to pray over their loved ones. (Read *The Watchman on The Wall: Daily Devotions for Praying God's Word* for examples.)

Step 21—Share in the Wonder of Talking Directly to God!

- Ask, did you ever think that you could talk to God like that? How great is God!

- Prepare for Week 4 – Big Step 22.

STEP 15—MORE WAYS TO TALK WITH GOD

☑ WEEK TWO

Congratulations—week two is now completed.

You learned how much Jesus loves you, about having a relationship with Him, and how to follow Him in obedience.

This week you will learn a variety of different types of prayers to help you talk with Him.

The Trinity is a word used to describe the union of God the Father, Jesus the Son, and the Holy Spirit as three Divine Persons in One God.

Prayer is a vital "stream" used by the Holy Spirit to help you grow and enjoy your relationship with God. Communicating is important to any working relationship. As oxygen is to the physical life, so prayer is to spiritual life. Prayer allows the Holy Spirit to work in you making you stronger. More importantly, prayer is the singular most important way you communicate with God.

Pray with your shepherd to start your time together:

"Lord, You are great! Thank You for loving me. Thank You for forgiving me. I give You this time to teach me Your will and ways. Help me to learn more about prayer today. In the name of Jesus I pray, Amen."

In the book of Matthew, Jesus was asked by His disciples to teach them to pray. In response, Jesus gave them this model prayer. Read Matthew 6:9-13.

⁹"Pray, then, in this way 'Our Father who is in heaven, Hallowed be Your name. ¹⁰Your kingdom come. Your will be done, on earth as it is in heaven. ¹¹Give us this day our daily bread. ¹²And forgive us our debts, as we also have forgiven our debtors. ¹³And do not lead us into temptation, but deliver us from evil. For Yours is the kingdom and the power and the glory forever. Amen.'"

Underline the names and pronouns for God.

Some people like to mark names of the Lord with a triangle showing Him as the head of the Trinity.

For example, "Our Father ..."

How many times did you mark names and pronouns for God? _____5_____

Now underline "us," "our," and "we." How many times did you underline them? ___9___

Work on memorizing this prayer this week. It is known as The Lord's Prayer. It is certainly not the only way to pray. In fact, God asks us not to recite prayers over and over thinking that repeating a prayer will make God more likely to answer that prayer.

Let us think about this prayer some more.

Do you have any questions or thoughts before we look at each line more closely?

_____

_____

The word "Hallowed" means holy.

What does holy mean to you?

God is holy: He is perfectly pure, immaculate, just, and good.

One of the types of prayers you will learn this week is called praise. God loves praise because it honors Him.

What other words in this prayer honor God?

Yours is the kingdom and the power and the glory forever.

Confession is where we come clean before the Lord. It is an admission of our guilt and precedes us asking God for His mercy and forgiveness.

Write what this prayer says about confession? (Some translations use the word trespasses instead of debts.)

Forgive us our debts, as we also have forgiven our debtors.

Are there lines about God's will being done? These are prayers of submission and intercession (asking for God to do something). List the ways God's will needs to be done:

"Your kingdom come. Your will be done, on earth as it is in heaven." God's kingdom needs to come. God's will needs to be done on earth as it is done in heaven.

Underline the areas where Jesus has you praying for assistance or help. List them below:

Give us this day our daily bread.

Lead us not into temptation.

Deliver us from evil.

⁹Pray then in this way,

"Our Father who is in heaven, Hallowed be Your name.

¹⁰Your kingdom come. Your will be done, on earth as it is in heaven.

¹¹Give us this day our daily bread. ¹²And forgive us our debts, as we also have forgiven our debtors.

¹³And do not lead us into temptation, but deliver us from evil.

For Yours is the kingdom and the power and the glory forever. Amen."

Matthew 6:9-13

"If we confess our sins, He is faithful and righteous to forgive us our sins and to cleanse us from all unrighteousness."

1 John 1:9

50 STEPS WITH JESUS   59

You are learning how to use verses from the Bible in your prayers for yourself and others. The Lord's Prayer is an example of a prayer from the Bible that you can pray. Pray with your shepherd this prayer for you, your loved ones, and your church.

"Our Father who is in heaven, hallowed be Your name. Your kingdom come. Your will be done, on earth as it is in heaven. Give us this day our daily bread. And forgive us our debts, as we also have forgiven our debtors. And do not lead us into temptation, but deliver us from evil. For Yours is the kingdom and the power and the glory forever. Lord, help me enjoy this week of talking to You more and in different ways! In the name of Jesus I pray, Amen."

As you are thinking about and praying these verses today, imagine Jesus' smile as you delight Him by letting Him work in your life through this prayer.

This is going to be a great week, a really great week!

STEP 16—TYPES OF PRAYER: THANKSGIVING

Dear new creation, "all things become new." Today you will learn and practice an important type of prayer. It is thanksgiving. Thanksgiving is both a way to express appreciation and an act of faith.

Earlier you studied 1 Thessalonians 5:16-18. Here are three habits of faith that can become constant in your life with the Lord's help: always rejoicing, unceasing prayer, and giving thanks in everything.

Take a look at the following verses from Philippians 4:6-7:

6Be anxious for nothing, but in everything by prayer and supplication with thanksgiving let your requests be made known to God. 7And the peace of God, which surpasses all comprehension, will guard your hearts and your minds in Christ Jesus.

What does anxious mean to you?

Anxious means to be troubled with cares, greatly concerned, or worried.

16Rejoice always; 17pray without ceasing; 18in everything give thanks; for this is God's will for you in Christ Jesus.

I THESSALONIANS 5: 16-18

How much are you supposed to be anxious about?

Nothing

How much should you bring to God in prayer?

Everything

What must be present with prayer and supplication (an intense request) for God to respond?

Thanksgiving

When true thanksgiving is present, one is thanking God in advance. It is an act of faith or trust.

Underline the Lord's promise in Philippians 4:6-7. Write out the benefits:

The peace of God, which surpasses all comprehension, will

guard your heart and your mind in Christ Jesus.

PRACTICE TIME:

Begin praying and thanking God. As you pray, list all of the things that you are thankful for and express your gratitude for them to the Lord.

Write them down if you would like.

Extra verses for reflection:

"Offer to God a sacrifice of thanksgiving and pay your vows to the Most High."
PSALM 50:14

*"Oh give thanks to the LORD, call upon His name;
make known His deeds among the peoples."*
PSALM 105:1

*"Oh give thanks to the LORD, for He is good,
for His lovingkindness is everlasting."*
PSALM 107:1

*"Devote yourselves to prayer, keeping alert in it
with an attitude of thanksgiving."*
COLOSSIANS 4:2

"Grow flowers of gratitude in the soil of prayer."

—Verbena Woods

STEP 17—TYPES OF PRAYER: PRAISE

Today you add to your prayers of appreciation to the Lord, prayers that adore Him for who He is. Thanksgiving usually focuses on God's actions, how He works in our lives, etc. Praise focuses on His person and His nature.

For example, you might say in the same prayer.

"Lord, thank You for making me. You are the Creator."

Go ahead and try it.

In thanksgiving, we are expressing our appreciation to God for what He has done, and in praise, our songs and words are to Him directly and are about who He is. This is very important in worship. God wants us to praise Him.

Sing praises to God, sing praises; sing praises to our King, sing praises.

PSALM 47:6

But as for me, I will declare it forever; I will sing praises to the God of Jacob.

PSALM 75:9

Enter His gates with thanksgiving and His courts with praise! Give thanks to Him; bless His name!

PSALM 100:4

Two missionaries, Paul and Silas, were falsely accused and imprisoned. Even while in jail they sang praises to God (Acts 16:16-26). This act of worship did not require the external circumstances of life to be good. These two men honored God by acknowledging Him despite their circumstances.

Look again at The Lord's Prayer from Step 15 (page 40).

Circle words that are statements of praise to God. Write those words here:

Hallowed is Your name.

Yours is the kingdom and the power and the glory forever.

What other words can you think of that describe who God is? Write them below:

Some examples are: Holy, Righteous, Faithful, All-powerful,

Just, Healer, Redeemer, Compassionate, Loving, Merciful,

Provider, Friend, Father, Beyond Compare, Indescribable!

THANKSGIVING

Expressing appreciation to God for what He has done.

PRAISE

Expressing the truths about who God is: His character and His nature.

Now pray these words to the Lord as an act of praise. "Lord, You are holy. You are ..."

_____

_____

_____

STEP 18—TYPES OF PRAYER: CONFESSION

Wow! God is great. One of the keys to your salvation and to your ongoing walk with the Lord is confession. Confession is prayer that helps us stay in a right relationship with God.

Pray,

"Lord, help me to pray sincerely when I need to confess my sins to You and accept Your forgiveness."

In The Lord's Prayer, what phrases talked about forgiveness?

Write the phrases here:

Forgive us our debts, as we also have forgiven our debtors.

_____

You have seen this verse before. It would be great to memorize it as well as Matthew 6:9-13. You will use it all of your life.

If we confess our sins, He is faithful and righteous to forgive us our sins and to cleanse us from all unrighteousness.

1 JOHN 1:9

A definition of Biblical confession is:

"Taking responsibility for personal sin, acknowledging it to God with true repentance, and receiving God's forgiveness in faith."

CONFESSION

Taking responsibility for personal sin, acknowledging it to God with true repentence, and receiving God's forgiveness in faith..

Read the verses below in your Bible to learn about these elements of confession:

1. God reveals your sin, often in quiet times of prayer (Psalm 51:1-3).

2. Tell the Lord you know that you are responsible for your sins. (Luke 18:9-14).

3. Jesus talked about the importance of repentance (Matthew 12:41). Repentance means to turn around completely into a new direction, like a u-turn.

4. Forgiveness must be accepted. Isaiah 1:18 teaches that there is no sin God will not forgive!

5. The result of confession is a right relationship with God. Psalm 51:10-13 really shows this truth.

Confession is a special time with God as you come to Him to deal with issues of sin in your life. Spend some time with the Lord. Ask Him to search your heart for unconfessed sin. (This is not a prayer of salvation, unless you have never asked the Lord to forgive your sins and be your Savior and Lord.)

REPENTENCE

The Greek word for repentance is metanoia. This literally means a change in one's way of life resulting from a spiritual conversion.

Metanoia is a change of mind and heart from which results a change in behavior.

STEP 19 — TYPES OF PRAYER: PETITION

Confession helps us stay in a right relationship with the Lord. A strong relationship with God is foundational for making specific requests for yourself and for others.

Petition is defined as: *"The act of lifting to God needs and desires of the heart with expectancy and faith in God for an answer."*

Pray and ask for help in learning how to petition—how to pray for things you need.

What in The Lord's Prayer (Step 15) sounds like petition?

Give us this day our daily bread

These are examples of prayer petitions from the Bible:

1. For Direction:

> *"… Let me know Your ways that I may know You, so that I may find favor in Your sight … If Your presence does not go with us, do not lead us up from here."*
>
> EXODUS 33:13-15

50 STEPS WITH JESUS

Learning to Walk Daily With the Lord

2. For Specific Requests:

> [14] *"This is the confidence which we have before Him, that, if we ask anything according to His will, He hears us. [15] And if we know that He hears us in whatever we ask, we know that we have the requests which we have from Him."*
>
> 1 JOHN 5:14-15

3. For Compassion:

> *"Remember, O LORD, Your compassion and Your lovingkindnesses, for they have been from of old."*
>
> PSALM 25:6

There is nothing too large or too small for us to lift to God in petition.

The key to successful petition is to pray for those things that are in God's will (1 John 5:14). For better effectiveness, spend time preparing your heart in thanksgiving, praise, and confession before you move into petition. These steps are certainly not required, but they are helpful. Often believers offer prayers of petition without ceasing throughout each day.

Are there some things on your heart that you would like to ask God about but have not asked Him as of yet. Go ahead! He wants you to talk with Him about everything.

If it helps, write them out:

_____

_____

_____

STEP 20—TYPES OF PRAYER: PRAYING FOR OTHERS

One of the great privileges and joys of being a Christian is the ability to bring to your loving Father concerns that you have for others. This type of prayer is known as intercessory prayer, but you can call it praying for others. It is a very important part of your prayer life to seek God for the sake of others.

Pray:

"Lord, help me learn how to pray for others. Please help me have Your heart for the needs of those around me."

As a new believer, you are probably very concerned about family and friends who need the Lord's blessings. Praying for them is a tool that God desires for you to use.

Here is some comfort in praying for others. The Holy Spirit is helping you.

[26]In the same way the Spirit also helps our weakness; for we do not know how to pray as we should, but the Spirit Himself intercedes for us with groanings too deep for words; [27]and He who searches the hearts knows what the mind of the Spirit is, because He intercedes for the saints according to the will of God.
ROMANS 8:26-27

Underline the word "Spirit" and then list the positive help the Holy Spirit gives you for praying.

The Spirit helps in our weakness.

The Spirit intercedes for us with groanings too deep for words.

He intercedes for the saints according to the will of God.

As you grow, you will learn you can pray for everyone: for non-Christians to become Christians, for enemies to change, for your country, for those you know who are going through a tough time and need to feel better.

Read below about how important praying for others is to God. Note the importance of doing this with the Lord's help (in the Spirit).

With all prayer and petition pray at all times in the Spirit, and with this in view, be on the alert with all perseverance and petition for all the saints.
EPHESIANS 6:18

List people that you have been praying for or need to pray for:

_____

_____

_____

_____

Go ahead and ask God to work in their lives. Pray for each of them individually.

Even when you don't know how to pray, the Holy Spirit prays for you. He makes intercession for you and prays God's will over you. What a comfort to know!

STEP 21 — TYPES OF PRAYER: CONVERSATIONAL

What an amazing week! The most important thing about prayer is that you are talking with God. In Step 4, you learned that God wants to spend time with you. He wants to talk with you all of the time! Pray:

"Lord, thank You for wanting to walk through this life with me! I love You. Help me to listen to You. I want to hear Your voice and know Your will."

Note these three great truths about having a conversation with God.

1. It is God's will for you to talk with Him all of the time. If He asks you to do it, then it is possible. Underline "pray without ceasing" and "this is God's will" in the verses below.

    ¹⁶Rejoice always; ¹⁷pray without ceasing; ¹⁸in everything give thanks; for this is God's will for you in Christ Jesus.
    1 THESSALONIANS 5:16-18

2. The Holy Spirit who lives in you is God's gift for you to understand Him. God will reveal Himself to you at your level of understanding.

    ¹²Now we have received, not the spirit of the world, but the Spirit who is from God, so that we may know the things freely given to us by God, ¹³which things we also speak, not in words taught by human wisdom, but in those taught by the Spirit, combining spiritual thoughts with spiritual words.
    1 CORINTHIANS 2:12-13

3. God wants you to draw close to Him. Time spent with God tunes your spiritual ear to hear His voice and know His heart.

    The secret of the LORD is for those who fear Him …
    PSALM 25:14

    There was reclining on Jesus' chest one of His disciples, whom Jesus loved.
    JOHN 13:23

God wants you to know Him. He gave you His Spirit to teach you about Him; He will reveal Himself to you as you draw close to Him.

There is a wonderful promise of knowing God and His will.

If you abide in Me, and My words abide in you, ask whatever you wish and it will be done for you.

John 15:7

What are your thoughts about these truths? What are your thoughts about what you have discovered in these verses?

_____

_____

_____

_____

_____

_____

_____

PRACTICING CONVERSATIONAL PRAYER

Spend some time talking and listening to God. As you pray, talk with God about wanting to be close to Him and about wanting to be able to understand His will for your life. Ask Him how to pray for yourself and others.

Conversational Prayer With Others

Praying <u>for</u> others is a blessing. Praying <u>with</u> other believers brings great joy and is one of the many benefits of knowing God and belonging to His family. The prayers of others strengthen you. As often as possible, connect with people who

love to pray together. You will find that being prayed for by others is a great blessing in your life. Praying for others out loud will also stretch and build your faith. When you encourage others, you are also encouraged!

You have already been praying with your shepherd. Tomorrow as you start your next week, make sure you pray together.

Practice your verses from Matthew 6:9-13 for tomorrow.

Another exciting week of walking with Jesus is ahead for you. Coming up you get to learn about the next stream of living Water—God's Word!

9Pray then in this way,

"Our Father who is in heaven, Hallowed be Your name.

10Your kingdom come. Your will be done, on earth as it is in heaven.

11Give us this day our daily bread. 12And forgive us our debts, as we also have forgiven our debtors.

13And do not lead us into temptation, but deliver us from evil.

For Yours is the kingdom and the power and the glory forever. Amen."

Matthew 6:9-13

WEEK FOUR

UNDERSTANDING THE BIBLE

All Scripture is inspired by God and is profitable for teaching, for reproof, for correction, for training in righteousness.

2 TIMOTHY 3:16

LESSON OVERVIEW—UNDERSTANDING THE BIBLE

The theme of this week is the second stream of living water—**the Word of God**.

Begin your time with prayer and answer any questions.

Cheer them on! As a review, have your student fill in the blanks with their own ideas about prayer. You can help them if they need it. Fill in the blanks for your life as well. The value of this exercise for memory is expanded if you are sincerely praying these prayers to the Lord.

Show them how to mark God and the pronouns for God with a triangle. If they want to use colored pencils or pens as they mark, they may choose any color for the triangle and the other symbols. Remind them that the "markings" are only suggestions. If there is a different symbol or color they want to use, that is super.

This is a powerful lesson with things that may be totally new to them. Enjoy walking them through the greatness of God's Word. Just like in the prayer lesson, describe what the Word of God means to you.

- Their memory verses this week will be 2 Timothy 3:16 and Psalm 1:1, 4-6.

- Have them share their memory verses from Week Three—Matthew 6:9-13 (Optional 1 John 1:9).

- Have them share their memory verses from Week Two—John 14:15 and 21.

- Have them share their memory verses from Week One—Psalm 1:2-3.

- Answer any questions and allow them the opportunity to just talk with you.

- Provide an overview of Steps 16-21. Each of these days will increase your ability to study and use God's Word. Some of these lessons may take a little longer this week, but the principles they learn will be very valuable for them as students of God's Word.

- Close in prayer.

Daily Prompts for Week 4
Steps 23-28—Understanding the Bible

Check in with your student each day to encourage them, to pray with them, and to continue developing your relationship with them. Here are some prompts that will help you as you connect with them each day.

Step 23—Tell them you are proud of them!

- Ask if they understand how reading the Bible is different than reading other books.

Step 24—Encourage them to use these tools as they study the Word.

- Share with them how these tools help see God's Word with great detail! Ask them what they learned from the Word in this lesson.

Step 25—Give support if they are struggling.

- God's Word is so rich and full of life. If your student is struggling with the study helps, reinforce that simply reading the Word is powerful. The tools are helpful and will enrich their understanding, but even simply reading the Bible will strengthen and encourage them.

- Follow up with them on the paragraph and chapter themes of the Bible. These are important, but if this is confusing or frustrating to them, encourage them to just keep reading. Underscore the value of meditating—even on a single verse—and remind them that they will grow in this area. Be patient with them and help them as they learn to use these valuable Bible study tools.

Step 26—Make sure they have a Bible to read from.

- Whether in print or electronic, make sure your student has acces to a Bible. If you are able, you might want to purchase a Bible for them as a gift, or perhaps your church will provide one. Having a Bible of their own they can mark in is the best option.

Step 27—Underscore the value of memorizing Scripture.

- This is a great lesson on memorizing Scripture. Hiding God's Word in our heart helps us to walk in grace and abandon sin.

Step 28—Celebrate them. Celebrate reaching this place.

- Ask them if they have a particular verse that has really spoken to them. Allow them to share what this verse means to them.

- Prepare for Week 5 – Big Step 29.

Learning to Walk Daily With the Lord

STEP 22—UNDERSTANDING THE BIBLE: INTRODUCTION

☑ WEEK THREE

Talking with God is one of the greatest blessings you will ever know.

Even when you struggle to find the right words, He knows your heart.

MEMORY VERSE

All Scripture is inspired by God and is profitable for teaching, for reproof, for correction, for training in righteousness.

2 Timothy 3:16

The Word of God is known as the Bible and Scripture. Sometimes Christians refer to individual lines in the Bible as scriptures or verses. More to follow in today's lesson.

Way to go! Week four is here. Isn't it great to talk with God? You have now learned many ways to talk with the Lord. Let's put them all together to start this new week. Use the following as a guide for your prayer together.

- *Lord, I thank You for* _____.

- *Lord, I praise You that You are* _____.

- *You are the Savior; search my heart for sin … (listen).*

- *Forgive me for* _____.

- *Dear Lord, help me with* _____.

- *Dear Lord, help* _____ *with their need of*

  _____.

- *Help me to learn how to listen to You and Your Word, so I can know You better. In the name of Jesus I pray.*

Today you begin to look at the second stream of the tree planted by running water. The first stream was prayer, and the second is the Word of God. The Holy Spirit loves to use the Word of God to help you grow and know the Lord better.

The "Word of God" refers to two things; one is the Bible, and the other is Jesus Himself. Jesus is the exact image of God who came to the earth to show us who God is and how much He loves us. God reveals Himself as Jesus. The Bible is also the revelation of God, but in written form. They are both holy and come from God.

So as a new believer, it is important for you to know why you need to understand your Bible and how to use your Bible. This is an exciting week.

Quote your memory verse from Psalm 1:2-3. What two words describe what the man is doing in verse 2?

Delights and meditates.

He is looking at the law of God. The "law of God" is often used to describe the entire Bible, but it also specifically refers to the first five books of the Bible found in a section called the Old Testament.

Look in your Bible and find the table of contents for the books of the Bible. (If you do not have a Bible yet, ask your shepherd to help you find one or how to use one online.)

What page is your table of contents on? _____.

50 STEPS WITH JESUS

Learning to Walk Daily With the Lord

Does it have both the Old and the New Testaments listed? _____

Some Bibles say Old Covenant and New Covenant. Keep this page number handy to help find the books of the Bible.

When Jesus was on earth, the New Testament was not yet written. People used only what we call the Old Testament. This Old Testament is the recording of God's work of love and forgiveness for mankind, and specifically for the children of Israel from creation until the rebuilding of Israel. It is vital for understanding the New Testament, which is about Jesus coming to earth to become your Savior and His promise to return to earth.

The Old Testament has 39 books in it, and the New Testament has 27. In order to be able to find particular Scriptures, chapters and verse numbers were added. So, as an example, your first memory verse this week is 2 Timothy 3:16:

All Scripture is inspired by God and is profitable for teaching, for reproof, for correction, for training in righteousness.

Have your shepherd show you how to find it in your Bible. Now find and read Psalm 1:1-6. *You may want to highlight or underline the verses to make them easier to locate again in the future.*

There are many reasons to invest your life in the Word of God. The man in Psalm 1 was changed because he spent time in the Word learning it. There are three important descriptions of Scripture in 2 Timothy 3:16 before the list *"for teaching, for reproof, for correction, for training in righteousness."*

Put a box around them and list them below:

1. ___All___ Scripture

2. is ___inspired___ by ___God___

3. and is ___profitable___.

Talk with your shepherd about why each description is important. These will be discussed tomorrow in your Day 23 study.

So you can understand the layout of the Old and New Testaments, look at the list of the Old Testament books of the Bible on this page. Follow along to see if you understand.

In the Old Testament books, Genesis through Esther are books of the history of the people of God. The first five of these books are often called the Law. The next set, Job to Lamentations, (with the exception of Isaiah and Jeremiah) is known as the wisdom literature. The final set, Isaiah to Malachi (with the exception of Lamentations) is known as prophecy.

Now look at the list of the New Testament books of the Bible on the following page.

OLD TESTAMENT BOOKS

Law
1. Genesis
2. Exodus
3. Leviticus
4. Numbers
5. Deuteronomy

History of the People of God
6. Joshua
7. Judges
8. Ruth
9. 1 Samuel
10. 2 Samuel
11. 1 Kings
12. 2 Kings
13. 1 Chronicles
14. 2 Chronicles
15. Ezra
16. Nehemiah
17. Esther

Wisdom Literature
18. Job
19. Psalm
20. Proverbs
21. Ecclesiastes
22. Song of Solomon

23. Isaiah ◄···Prophecy
24. Jeremiah ◄···
25. Lamentations

Prophecy
26. Ezekiel
27. Daniel
28. Hosea
29. Joel
30. Amos
31. Obadiah
32. Jonah
33. Micah
34. Nahum
35. Habakkuk
36. Zephaniah
37. Haggai
38. Zechariah
39. Malachi

NEW TESTAMENT BOOKS

History of Jesus
Gospels

1. Matthew
2. Mark
3. Luke
4. John
5. Acts ......

History of the early church

6. Romans
7. 1 Corinthians
8. 2 Corinthians
9. Galatians
10. Ephesians
11. Philippians
12. Colossians
13. 1 Thessalonians
14. 2 Thessalonians
15. 1 Timothy
16. 2 Timothy
17. Titus
18. Philemon
19. Hebrews
20. James
21. 1 Peter
22. 2 Peter
23. 1 John
24. 2 John
25. 3 John
26. Jude
27. Revelation

Pastoral Letters

Prophecy

In the New Testament, the first five books are history as well; the first four are about Jesus' life, and the book of Acts is about the history of the early church. The next set, Romans to Jude, is called pastoral letters. The final book, Revelation, is prophecy.

It would be wonderful for you to begin reading any one of these books. Talk it over with your shepherd. Some people start with a book about Jesus, others begin with Genesis, still others choose Proverbs or Psalms as a great place to create the habit of daily reading. You can't go wrong. Please understand that the Bible is unlike any book ever written. It is God's Word, and it is living (Hebrews 4:12). As you read, the Holy Spirit in you will help you understand.

Get a Bible you are not afraid to write in. Underline passages that speak to you, make notes in the margins, draw shapes over certain words as you are learning to do in this study. Personalize verses by adding your name to specific promises you discover while reading. The Bible is your roadmap to walking daily with your Savior. It is God's love letter and guidebook to you. He loves when you make it your own.

But the helper, the Holy Spirit, whom the Father will send in My name, He will teach you all things …

JOHN 14:26

The Bible is going to come alive as the Lord reveals things to you.

Pray:

God, open my eyes and heart to Your Word!

———⊰⊱———

STEP 23 — UNDERSTANDING THE BIBLE THE INSPIRED WORD

This is an exciting day. Ask God to help you see Him in the Word.

Here is your memory verse again from 2 Timothy 3:16:

All Scripture is inspired by God and is profitable for teaching, for reproof, for correction, for training in righteousness.

Put a box around the focus phrases you found yesterday about Scripture.

- "**ALL**" – is very important because it does not give us the opportunity to decide which Bible verses are from God and which ones are not. If we were to choose, we would miss out and make the Bible fit our thoughts rather than helping shape our thoughts to God's.

- "**INSPIRED**" – this word means "given and breathed out by God." While written by human hands, the source of the Bible is God. Note this passage from 2 Peter 1:20-21.

[20]But know this first of all, that no prophecy of Scripture is a matter of one's own interpretation, [21]for no prophecy was ever made by an act of human will, but men moved by the Holy Spirit spoke from God.

- **"PROFITABLE"** – This is a great word to consider when thinking about investing your time and life in the Lord's Word. Profit means you get more out of it than you invest in it. The Bible is a dynamic, powerful book.

For the word of God is living and active and sharper than any two-edged sword, and piercing as far as the division of soul and spirit, of both joints and marrow, and able to judge the thoughts and intentions of the heart.

HEBREWS 4:12

A lady in East Africa carried her Bible under her arm everywhere she went. Her friends teased her and said, "Aren't there any other books you could read?" She said, "Yes, but this is the only book that reads me."

Reading the Bible is a great part of walking with Jesus. Talk with Him as you read His Word and listen as He helps you understand it.

Pray for those who God has laid upon your heart today.

In addition to memorizing 2 Timothy 3:16, work on memorizing the rest of Psalm 1 for this week. You have two of the six verses already memorized!

STEP 24 — UNDERSTANDING THE BIBLE
HOW TO STUDY: PART 1

Pray with thankfulness to the Lord for His gift of the Bible.

For the next two days you will learn how to use eight tools for mining the Word of God to discover the wealth of gems it contains. Today you will practice using four of the tools.

1. KEYWORDS:

These are repeated words or phrases that unlock the meaning of what you are reading. God, Jesus, and Holy Spirit are always keywords in the Bible. You get to read God's Word to get to know God!

50 STEPS
WITH JESUS

Learning to Walk Daily With the Lord

Like you did in Step 15, put a triangle around "LORD" and the pronoun "His" that refers to LORD in Psalm 1 printed below.

The LORD has a law. The LORD wants us to meditate on His law day and night.

=

The LORD knows the way of the righteous.

=

¹*How blessed is the man who does not walk in the counsel of the wicked, nor stand in the path of sinners, nor sit in the seat of scoffers!* ²*But his delight is in the law of the LORD, and in His law he meditates day and night.* ³*He will be like a tree firmly planted by streams of water, which yields its fruit in its season and its leaf does not wither; and in whatever he does, he prospers.* ⁴*The wicked are not so, but they are like chaff which the wind drives away.* ⁵*Therefore the wicked will not stand in the judgment, nor sinners in the assembly of the righteous.* ⁶*For the LORD knows the way of the righteous, but the way of the wicked will perish.*

What do you learn about God from this psalm? Record your answers in the "Questions and Reflections" column next to the verses where you marked the words "LORD" and "His."

2. LISTS:

Look for lists within the chapter. For example, Psalm 1:1-2 lists Godly characteristics of someone who is blessed.

Put a "1" over "does not walk in the counsel of the wicked." Place a "2" over "nor stand in the path of sinners," etc. You should find and number 5 characteristics.

What do you learn about the blessed person?

1. He does not walk in the counsel of the wicked.

2. He does not stand in the path of sinners.

3. He does not sit in the seat of scoffers.

4. He delights in the law of the LORD.

5. He meditates on God's law day and night.

3. CONTRASTS:

Mark contrasts within the chapter. Many times a contrast will be indicated by "but" or "however".

Mark contrasts with a lightning bolt symbol like this. ⚡

Learning to Walk Daily With the Lord

Put a lightning bolt in front of "but" in Psalm 1:2 and 4. What do you learn from those contrasts?

Instead of being with sinners, the blessed person is delighting in

God's law and meditating on it day and night.

The wicked are not like the blessed person who is firmly planted;

they are like wind-driven chaff.

4. COMPARISONS:

Mark comparisons within the chapter. Comparisons refer to things that are similar and will often be indicated by the words "like" or "as".

Circle "like" in Psalm 1:3-4. Put an equal sign = in front of verses that contain comparisons. What do you learn from those comparisons?

A righteous person is like a fruit bearing tree firmly planted by

streams of water who will not wither.

A wicked person is like wind-driven chaff.

Thank God for making you a blessed person and for teaching you how to study His Bible.

STEP 25 — UNDERSTANDING THE BIBLE HOW TO STUDY: PART 2

Pray:

*"Lord, help me learn to study Your Word better,
so I can know You better."*

Yesterday, you learned four tools for studying God's Word. List those tools below:

1. Keywords .
2. Lists .
3. Contrasts .
4. Comparisons .

Today, you will learn four more tools for studying the Bible. They are:

5. EXPRESSIONS OF TIME:

Mark words that show time, timing of events, or sequence of events. Look for words like "then," "when," "after," "until" besides obvious time words like "day and night."

Go back to Psalm 1 printed on page 56.
Draw a clock over "day and night" in Psalm 1 like this.

What do you learn from marking that time phrase? When are you supposed to be thinking about God's Word?

You should be thinking about God's Word all the time.

6. TERMS OF CONCLUSION/RESULT/PURPOSE:

Mark words like "therefore," "because," "for," "so that," "for this reason." These words indicate a conclusion or a result that happened.

Mark terms of conclusion with a triangle of dots like this.

Terms of conclusion will answer why and how questions.

Put a triangle of dots around "therefore" in Psalm 1:5. Why will the wicked not stand in the judgment nor be in the assembly of the righteous?

The wicked will be driven away like chaff because they do not delight in the things of God.

Put a triangle of dots around "for" in Psalm 1:6. Why will the righteous be able to stand in the judgment and be in the assembly of the righteous?

Because the Lord knows them, they will stand and be in the assembly of the righteous. ("Know" in Hebrew is "yada": to intimately know.)

7. PARAGRAPH THEMES:

Write out themes that you find within Bible chapters. This will help you grasp what God wants to teach you in each chapter.

What are verses 1-3 about from Psalm 1?

The blessed man

(Paragraph and chapter themes do not need to be long. They should be enough words for you to remember what the paragraph and chapter are about. It is, however, okay if you want to write a brief paragraph summary.)

What do these symbols represent to you as you study the Word?

What are verses 4-6 about from Psalm 1?

The wicked

---

8. CHAPTER THEMES:

After you study a chapter from a book of the Bible, write a theme for the chapter. Writing your own chapter themes helps you remember what you studied.

What is your chapter theme for Psalm 1? Share or discuss this with your shepherd.

The blessed/righteous person contrasted with the wicked,

sinners, and scoffers

Thank God for giving you tools to study His Word and find the treasures He wants to share with you. Ask God to give you the desire to read and learn His Word for the rest of your life.

STEP 26 — UNDERSTANDING THE BIBLE YOU AND THE WORD!

Having time with God in His Word every day is a great part of the believer's life. You have added eight tools for studying the Word into your life! Today you will discover ways you can apply them to your studies and add the Word to your life.

Be diligent to present yourself approved to God as a workman who does not need to be ashamed, accurately handling the word of truth.

2 TIMOTHY 2:15

Pray:

"Lord, as Your Word is a lifetime of learning, help me to enjoy each day what You reveal to me, so I can grow."

A Bible study is regular time in the Word with a purpose.

1. Materials:

    a. A Bible and a notebook are what you need.

2. A Type of Study:

    a. Book Study: Going through a book or chapter of the Bible verse by verse.

    b. Word or Topical Study: Looking at a specific word or topic in the Bible (love, fear, forgiveness, marriage).

    c. Character Study: Looking at a specific person or entity (Abraham, Jesus, etc.).

3. A Bible Study Method:

    a. Prayer – Ask the Holy Spirit to teach you as you study His Word.

    b. Observation – Observing precisely what the verses say. Observation is what you learned to do on steps 24-25.

    c. Interpretation – Understanding what the verses mean.

    d. Application – The final step is asking the Lord 'What do the verses mean personally to me? How will I apply the truth to my life?'

Your church should have many Bible studies to help the congregation grow. If there are not any where you live, ask your shepherd to help you find one.

One of the greatest things you are learning in your 50 Steps is that you and the Lord can walk together in prayer and the Word on your own when other believers are not around. You can begin a Bible study from your daily readings or from your memory verses.

Pray:

Lord, help me to be a lifelong lover of Your Word! Help me to find You and myself in it. Help me to be a workman unashamed, handling your Word accurately.

Is there a specific book of the Bible you feel drawn to or curious about? Is there a specific topic you want to learn more about? How about a character from the Bible … Old Testament or New?

Which of these types of Bible study most interest you?

Talk this over with your shepherd and choose a study to work through, perhaps together or even with a group!

STEP 27 — UNDERSTANDING THE BIBLE MEMORIZING

A great tool to remain as a tree firmly planted by streams of water (Psalm 1:3) is to memorize God's Word. While you are already doing this, this step explains why and may give you more ideas for how to memorize the Word.

*But his delight is in the law of the LORD,
and in His law he meditates day and night.*

PSALM 1:2

Look up these verses and read why you memorize Scripture:

1. Our Lord has commanded it (Joshua 1:8).

2. It gives us a tool to combat sin (Psalm 119:9-11).

3. It gives food for your daily walk (Matthew 4:4).

How to Memorize Scripture

The keys are commitment and consistency.

1. Memorize the Word perfectly by reference, verse, reference. For example say:

   "2 Timothy 3:16: All Scripture is inspired by God and profitable for teaching, for reproof, for correction, for training in righteousness. 2 Timothy 3:16."

2. Read the verse in context and meditate on its meaning.

3. Memorize by phrases, and let the punctuation help you.

4. Write the verses out in a journal or on notecards that you can carry with you.

5. Repetition is the key. Say the verse 300 times for solid memory.

Our verses for these past 4 weeks are:

1. Psalms 1:2-3

2. John 14:15, 21

3. Matthew 6:9-13

4. 1 John 1:9 *(Optional)*

5. Psalms 1:1, 4-6

6. 2 Timothy 3:16

Practice memorizing all of your verses because Step 29 is around the corner!

Are you experiencing any struggles with memorizing? Is something blocking you from learning them; do you feel distracted when you go to work on them?

This is not meant to be legalistic, and there is no standard of performance you need to feel like you must achieve. Memorizing Scripture does not make you a worthy Christian. The whole purpose of memorizing verses is to write them on the tablet of your heart. As you memorize, you meditate. It gets the Word down deep into your spirit and washes it over your soul as it renews your mind.

Talk with your shepherd about any difficulties you may be having. Pray for the Lord to help you memorize the Word and see Him more clearly through this practice. It is a discipline worth developing.

STEP 28 — UNDERSTANDING THE BIBLE PRAYING THE WORD

Pray:

"Lord, help me pray today using Your Bible as a tool."

Today is a great day. You will learn to pray the Word of the Lord as a part of your prayer requests. See in these verses that praying with the Word of God is a great prayer tool.

[17]And take the helmet of salvation, and the sword of the Spirit, which is the Word of God. [18]With all prayer and petition pray at all times in the Spirit, and with this in view, be on the alert with all perseverance and petition for all the saints.
EPHESIANS 6:17-18

This week you learned about God's Word and how to mine its treasures so you can know who God is and how to live in an intimate and righteous relationship with Him. As you learn God's Word, you can also pray His Words back to Him for yourself and others. Praying Bible verses helps you pray with confidence because you are saying the very Words of God that contain God's will.

You spent two days studying Psalm 1. You know it is God's will for you and your loved ones to be righteous people who walk with the LORD. Psalm 1 is a great chapter to pray over yourself and those you love. It is printed below as a prayer to the LORD. Insert your loved ones' names into the blank, and pray for them and yourself.

"LORD, I want my family to be blessed by You.

Please do not let _____ and me walk in the counsel of the wicked, nor stand in the path of sinners, nor sit in the seat of scoffers. Let us delight in Your law, LORD, and meditate on it day and night. Let us be like a tree firmly planted by streams of water which yields its fruit in its season and whose leaf does not whither. Let us prosper in whatever we do. Do not let us be wicked. We do not want to be like chaff which the wind drives away. We want to stand in the judgment and be in the assembly of the righteous. LORD, You know the way of the righteous.

Make us Your righteous people. Do not let us perish.

In Your name, Jesus~ "

Now you try it. Psalm 54:4 says:

> *Behold, God is my helper; the Lord is the sustainer of my soul.*

Say it back to Him as a prayer:

> *"God, be my* <u>helper</u> *and the sustainer of* <u>my soul</u> *."*

This is exciting! Week four has equipped you to be able to more confidently open God's Word, walk with Him in it, and use it for prayer for others!

SUMMARY

From Week 3 you have learned:

- **Step 15**— Prayer is a vital "stream" used by the Holy Spirit to help you grow and enjoy your relationship with God. There are many types of prayer.

- **Step 16**—The prayer of **thanksgiving** expresses appreciation and is also an act of faith toward God. These prayers focus on God's actions, what He has done.

- **Step 17**—The prayer of **praise** expresses our appreciation for who God is, His character and His nature.

- **Step 18**—The prayer of **confession** helps us stay in right relationship with God. Confession is taking responsibility for personal sin, acknowledging it to God with true repentence, and receiving God's forgiveness in faith.

- **Step 19**—The prayer of **petition** is the act of lifting to God needs and desires of the heart with expectancy and faith in God for an answer.

- **Step 20**—The prayer of intercession is simply **praying for others**. It is the ability to bring to your loving Father concerns that you have for others.

- **Step 21**—**Conversational prayers** are you talking with God about absolutely anything. They allow your relationship with Him to develop and strengthen as He reveals Himself to you and brings you greater understanding of Himself and His Word.

From Week 4 you have learned:

- **Step 22**—The Word is the Bible, and it is Jesus. Understanding the Word is crucial to having a meaningful walk with God.

- **Step 23**—The Scripture is inspired by the Holy Spirit and all of it is profitable to us as believers.

- **Step 24**—Understanding the Bible is easier when you use tools to help you better comprehend its meaning. Some tools we learned to use are:

    1. keywords

    2. lists

    3. contrasts

    4. comparisons

- **Step 25**—Some additional tools for studying the Bible we developed are:

    5. paying attention to expressions of time

    6. terms of conclusion, result, or purpose

    7. paragraph themes

    8. chapter themes

- **Step 26**—We talked about Bible studies focused on a specific book, word or topic, or character in the Bible. As a method of study, we employ prayer, observation, interpretation, and application.

- **Step 27**—Memorizing Scripture is a wonderful way to increase our understanding of God's Word. As we hide God's Word in our hearts, we walk in righteousness and forsake sin.

- **Step 28**—Praying the Word of God is a powerful tool. As we pray God's Word back to Him, we pray confidently in agreement with His will.

Write down two or three key things which have had the greatest impact on you the last two weeks of your journey.

_____

_____

_____

_____

_____

_____

_____

WEEK FIVE

BEING PART OF THE CHURCH

And let us consider how to stimulate one another to love and good deeds, not forsaking our own assembling together, as is the habit of some, but encouraging one another, and all the more as you see the day drawing near.

HEBREWS 10:24-25

SHEPHERD'S GUIDE
BIG STEP 29

LESSON OVERVIEW—BEING PART OF THE CHURCH

The theme of this week is the third stream of living water—**the church.** One of the great blessings of being a believer is belonging to the family of God, and spending time together with "immediate" family in a local church is a great way to be strengthened in the Lord.

Begin your time with prayer and answer any questions.

Mark together the words "God" and "Jesus" as before. Help them think of a marking for the Holy Spirit.

- Have a strategy for helping your student integrate into your church if they have not already.

- They will need to be on the path to membership if they have not joined.

- Think about where they can begin to serve.

This is a powerful lesson with things that may be totally new to your student. Enjoy walking them through the greatness of God's church. Just like in the prayer and Word lessons, describe what the church means to you.

- Their memory verses for this week will be—1 Corinthians 3:16 and Hebrews 10:24-25.

- Have them share their memory verses from Week Four—2 Timothy 3:16 and Psalm 1:1, 4-6

- Have them share their memory verses from Week Three—Matthew 6:9-13 (Optional 1 John 1:9)

- These were their memory verses from Week Two—John 14:15 and 21.

- These were their memory verses from Week One—Psalm 1:2-3.

- Answer any questions and allow them the opportunity to just talk with you.

- Give an overview of Steps 30-35. Each of these days will increase their ability to be a great part of the church family.

- Close in prayer.

Daily Prompts for Week 5
Steps 30-35—Being Part of The Church

Check in with your student each day to encourage them, to pray with them, and to continue developing your relationship with them. Here are some prompts that will help you as you connect with them each day.

Step 30—Tell Them You Are Proud of Them!

- Ask what they thought about this life-changing truth from 1 Corinthians 3:16.

Step 31—Remind Them That They Have Gifts From God.

- Ask if they found all of the gifts and if they have any questions. The 20 spiritual gifts from 1 Corinthians 12:8-10, 28; Romans 12:6-8; Ephesians 4:11-12. (The full list is provided for you on page 113).

Step 32—Congratulate Them on Being "Saints."

- Ask about Jesus being the foundation of their lives.

- Ask if there is a part of their lives He is not the foundation of yet.

Step 33—Think of Something Special About Your Student and Tell Them.

- Ask them what they think about the church being His bride. Make sure they are clear about this concept and understand the all-encompassing, everlasting love He has for them.

Step 35—Encourage Their Service in Their Church.

- Ask if they have any questions (or even concerns) about church.

- Ask if they feel like they belong and are beginning to feel at home in their church.

Step 36—Celebrate Their Progress.

- Ask what they think about being part of a group of people who love each other.

- Ask if there is anything thus far that does not make sense to them.

- Prepare for Week 6 – Big Step 37.

STEP 29 — BEING A PART OF THE CHURCH INTRODUCTION

Congratulations! You have completed Week 4 and are now moving into Week 5! Last week you learned that God uses our conversations with Him and His Word to help us be in an active relationship with Him and grow in our faith.

You identified in Week 1 that prayer and the Word are two of the "Streams of Water" that nourishes the tree in Psalm 1. Now you will learn how to walk with Jesus as you learn about the third stream, the church.

Pray:

> *"Lord, thank You that I get to talk with You and walk with You.*
> *Thank You for Your Bible—Your Word—so I can learn even more*
> *about You. This week help me learn more about Your church.*
> *In Your name, Jesus, I pray. Amen."*

The church is marvelous! The word "church" means "called out assembly." It is a picture of believers who have left the world's people group and joined God's people group. The word church is used to describe a single local group of believers. It is also used to describe the large group made up of all believers around the world. You, as a Christian, are part of the big global Church. The Lord wisely uses the local church to help individuals grow and worship Him.

This week we'll discover many things about the local church. The Bible uses three great pictures to describe the church: the **body**, the **building**, and the **bride**.

In 1 Corinthians 12:27 you read:

> *Now you are Christ's body and individually members of it.*

As an individual, you are part of a diversely gifted community. Look at 1 Corinthians 12:4-7 to see why it is diverse.

> *⁴Now there are varieties of gifts, but the same Spirit. ⁵And there are varieties of ministries, and the same Lord. ⁶There are varieties of effects, but the same God who works all things in all persons. ⁷But to each one is given the manifestation of the Spirit for the common good.*

Mark the Spirit as you like, and Lord (Jesus) and God as you have before. Write below what each one does:

SPIRIT:

The Spirit has a variety of gifts. Each believer is given a
manifestation of the Spirit for the common good. In other words,
we use the gift(s) given to us by the Spirit for the good of others.

MEMORY VERSE

Do you not know that you are a temple of God, and that the Spirit of God dwells in you?

1 Corinthians 3:16

LORD:

The Lord has a variety of ministries. (Believers use the gifts given

by the Spirit to help in the Lord's ministries.)

GOD:

God has a variety of effects that He works out in believers as they

use their spiritual gifts in the Lord's ministries.

How involved is God in the process gifting people for ministry?

God is totally involved! His Spirit provides the gift to the believer that the Lord Jesus needs for

His ministry. God the Father is responsible for the effects of that ministry in the lives of people.

Now read 1 Corinthians 12:7-20. What do you learn from this passage?

God uses the analogy of a human body to help you understand His church. Just as a human body

has many parts and they are all vitally important, so does the body of Christ have many members,

and they are all vitally important. The church needs every member using their spiritual gift(s) in

order to function properly.

List the four body parts.

foot	hand
ear	eye

This illustration of the body is used to help local church members understand the need for God to disperse spiritual gifts throughout congregations for His purposes.

Read 1 Corinthians 12:18 again.

A spiritual gift is an ability you are given by God when you become a Christian in order to help serve other members of your church. Every Christian has at least one. As you walk with the Lord, grow as a Christian, and serve in your church, your gift(s) will become evident to others and to yourself.

Spiritual gifts are not based on your talents or personality. They are supernatural. Spiritual gifts are evidenced when you practice them with the Lord. When you discover your gift(s), you will be able to supernaturally minister to others. It will be obvious it is the Lord working through you.

This week you will learn more about spiritual gifts and other great Holy Spirit benefits to being a believer and part of the body of Christ, the church.

A SPIRITUAL GIFT is a supernatural ability given to you by God when you become a Christian.

God gives spiritual gifts to us in order to help us serve others.

Learning to Walk Daily With the Lord

If you have not already connected to a local assembly, your shepherd will help you find one and become a part!

Discuss with your shepherd the value of the church in our lives as believers.

As you finish, pray for God to bless your church, help you become a dynamic part of it, and help you discover your spiritual gift(s).

Memorize 1 Corinthians 3:16:

> *Do you not know that you are a temple of God,*
> *and that the Spirit of God dwells in you?*

STEP 30 — BEING A PART OF THE CHURCH THE HOLY SPIRIT IN YOU

MEMORY VERSE

Do you not know that you are a temple of God, and that the Spirit of God dwells in you?

1 Corinthians 3:16

This is another exciting day! Ask God to help you see His Holy Spirit working in your life.

Continue working on your memory verse, 1 Corinthians 3:16.

This is a great verse. The Jewish temple in Jerusalem was torn down by the Romans in 70 A.D. This was about 40 years after Jesus was crucified, buried, resurrected, and had ascended to heaven. Jesus said the temple would be torn down, and He would rebuild it in three days. He was talking about the three days of His death and resurrection. The old temple would no longer be needed for righteousness since Jesus is the perfect sacrifice.

As Jesus ascended to heaven to be in the heavenly temple with God, He performed a miracle in the lives of people. As a part of people becoming Christians, they get to have the Holy Spirit living in them. Therefore, the new temple is you!

Interestingly, this Scripture was written about 15 years before the Romans tore down the temple in Jerusalem. Jesus started making Christians and His new temple on the earth very soon after He went to heaven.

Here are a few other benefits of having the Holy Spirit in you. Look up and read the following verses (in parenthesis) and ask the Holy Spirit to help you understand His Words.

- *He is the giver and power of God for the spiritual gifts* (1 Corinthians 12:4-7).

- *He produces Spiritual fruit in your life* (Galatians 5:22-23).

- *He comforts, counsels, and abides in you* (John 14:16-17).

- *He helps you in prayer* (Romans 8:26).

- *He convicts you of sin* (John 16:8).

Pray:

> *"Holy Spirit, fill my life with You. Help me bear Your wonderful fruit.*
> *Thank You for loving me and helping me pray.*
> *Help me use my spiritual gift. In Jesus' name I pray. Amen."*

Pray for others you know who need the Holy Spirit's work in their lives.

STEP 31 — BEING A PART OF THE CHURCH THE BODY

Pray for God to help you understand His illustration of the body even more.

On Step 29, you read 1 Corinthians 12:12-20 where the illustration of the body as the church was introduced. Today, reread 1 Corinthians 12:12-20 and continue through verse 31.

What do you think was happening for Paul to write this passage of the Bible?

There was jealousy among the members of the church in Corinth.
Some people thought their spiritual gift was not as important as
another person's. Some thought they didn't need other members of
their church. This wrong thinking was creating division in the church.

Some people were receiving spiritual gifts that they felt were less than other people's spiritual gifts. So Paul wrote to help them realize that all parts of the body are important, and the church should function as a unit and not a bunch of different body parts.

What is encouraging about verses 22-26? (List what you find below.)

Every member of the church is important. God has chosen which
person will receive which spiritual gift for His purposes.

Paul lists several spiritual gifts in 1 Corinthians 12:8-10 and 28.

Number them in your Bible then list them below: *(The gifts of healing, miracles, prophecy, and tongues are listed twice in verses 9-10 and verse 28. You only need to write them once.)*

1. Word of wisdom
2. Word of knowledge
3. Faith
4. Healing
5. Miracles
6. Prophecy
7. Distinguishing of spirits
8. Tongues
9. Interpretation of tongues
10. Apostle
11. Teacher
12. Helps
13. Administration

BONUS

What seven spiritual gifts are listed in Romans 12:6-8?
1. Prophecy
2. Service
3. Teaching
4. Exhortation
5. Giving
6. Leadership
7. Mercy

DOUBLE BONUS

Five spiritual gifts are listed in Ephesians 4:11-12. Two of these are not listed in the verses from 1 Corinthians and Romans. What are these two spiritual gifts?
1. Evangelist
2. Pastor

You can discover the other seven spiritual gifts in Romans 12:6-8 and Ephesians 4:11-12. All together, there are 20 spiritual gifts.

Write a single sentence about what 1 Corinthians 12 is about:

Spiritual gifts are given, controlled, and powered by God for the sake of His church, the body of Christ.

Ask God to bless your church with unity and harmony, so it can care for one another well. Consider how your spiritual gift(s) can serve your church family.

Step 32 — Being a Part of the Church
The Building

Pray:

*"Lord, help me learn to study Your Word better
so I can know You better."*

Another illustration for the church is a building. This is another great way to understand the church and how important you are to it.

Read Ephesians 2:19-22 below and mark God, Jesus, and the Spirit. Circle the words that apply to you.

19So then you are no longer strangers and aliens, but you are fellow citizens with the saints, and are of God's household, 20having been built on the foundation of the apostles and prophets, Christ Jesus Himself being the cornerstone, 21in whom the whole building, being fitted together, is growing into a holy temple in the Lord, 22in whom you also are being built together into a dwelling of God in the Spirit.

What from these verses applies to you? Make your list below:

1. You are no longer strangers and aliens.

2. You are fellow citizens with the saints.

3. You are of God's household.

4. You are being built together into a dwelling of God in the Spirit.

Are you a saint? The answer is that all authentic Christians are saints to the Lord. Being a saint means that by believing in Jesus you have been made holy by His blood.

Your Savior is the cornerstone of the church. How about your life? Jesus is also the cornerstone of your life. Ponder that truth. Jesus is the foundation stone for your life. Let Jesus build your life on Him.

You don't become a saint by being good or by doing good things. <u>All</u> authentic Christians are saints to the Lord.

You are holy because He is holy, and He now lives in you … His temple!

STEP 33 — BEING A PART OF THE CHURCH THE BRIDE

Pray today for the Lord's blessings upon you as you see Him as the groom and the church as His bride.

In the future, the Lord will return to get His bride. It is a beautiful picture of our relationship as an entire church with Jesus. At the end of the lesson there are two new memory verses to learn and meditate on.

Read Revelation 22:16-17 and see the church as the bride joining with the Holy Spirit to encourage people to experience Jesus.

In John 3:29, John the Baptist tells people who Jesus is and says,

> *"He who has the bride is the bridegroom; but the friend of the bridegroom, who stands and hears him, rejoices greatly because of the bridegroom's voice. So this joy of mine has been made full."*

The following two memory verses are great and really help set the stage for how to think about being a dynamic local church member. The final phrase encourages believers who are waiting for the day when the groom returns for His bride.

> *24And let us consider how to stimulate one another to love and good deeds, 25not forsaking our own assembling together, as is the habit of some, but encouraging one another, and all the more as you see the day drawing near.*
> HEBREWS 10:24-25

As you look at the above verses, apply some of your newly developed Bible study tools to this passage.

Mark the list of commands in Hebrews 10:24-25. How many did you find?

_____3_____

Write them below:

1. Consider how to stimulate one another to love and good deeds.

2. Do not forsake assembling together.

3. Encourage one another more and more.

MEMORY VERSES

24And let us consider how to stimulate one another to love and good deeds,

25not forsaking our own assembling together, as is the habit of some, but encouraging one another, and all the more as you see the day drawing near.

Hebrews 10:24-25

Why do you think these commands are an important part of a local church's health?

These commands help us keep each other strong in the Lord.

They keep us doing the things the Lord wants us to do.

_____

_____

You are a part of the bride. Brides know who they are. Brides are getting ready for the groom to come. On their wedding day, they want to be the most beautiful they have ever been. They want to be in the best shape of their lives. They don't want to disappoint the groom. These same ideas apply to individuals who are part of churches and to the churches themselves.

Pray:

"Lord, I want You to be proud of me. Make me beautiful in Your eyes."

STEP 34 — BEING A PART OF THE CHURCH PLUGGING IN

Pray:

"Jesus, help me be active in my church and be a servant of others."

Being a part of the church is often difficult if a person has not grown up in one. Lots of things do not make sense. In fact, spend a few minutes and write down some things that you want to ask your shepherd about your church:

_____

_____

_____

_____

_____

_____

What are some of the things you are supposed to do from the Hebrews 10:24-25 memory verses? Write the verses below. As you write, ask God to help you obey what He says to do in these verses.

_____

_____

_____

_____

_____

_____

_____

_____

Underline the commands in the verses you wrote.

Do you have anyone in your life whom you are spurring on, inviting to church, or encouraging? Hebrews 10:24-25 reminds us to plug-in and to serve. Another way to describe what every believer needs to do is to "connect" or "belong."

Remember the passage below when Jesus washed the disciple's feet in Step 14?

> *12So when He had washed their feet, and taken His garments and reclined at the table again, He said to them, "Do you know what I have done to you? 13You call Me Teacher and Lord; and you are right, for so I am. 14If I then, the Lord and the Teacher, washed your feet, you also ought to wash one another's feet. 15For I gave you an example that you also should do as I did to you."*
> JOHN 13:12-15

In order to minister to others, you have to want to serve others and you have to plug-in. Ask your shepherd for help in plugging into the right places in your church.

Pray for the Lord to help you find the right places to serve and be more like Jesus.

Joining a church family will help you connect meaningfully with other believers.

This provides you with a vital link for strength, companionship, growth, and encouragement. It allows you to belong.

Serving others is a rich blessing!

STEP 35 — BEING A PART OF THE CHURCH THE FAMILY

Pray:

"Father, thank You that I get to be a part of Your family. Thank You for the Spirit inside of me, for Jesus, my big brother, and for giving me this church family on the earth. I love You. Help me be a great family member to others."

This is the last day of your focus on the church. This is one of the streams of water from Psalm 1 that the Holy Spirit uses to help you always bear fruit in season and never wither.

One great way to connect and become involved is to find a small group or a Bible study where you can get to know people well and love them as they love you. Even if you attend a large church, there are probably many small groups meeting. Make friends and family with them. Talk with your shepherd if you have any questions about how to do this.

When you are involved, love the people of your church. Jesus said in John 13:34-35:

³⁴A new commandment I give to you, that you love one another, even as I have loved you, that you also love one another. ³⁵By this all men will know that you are My disciples, if you have love for one another.

At the end of the story about the church being a body in 1 Corinthians 12, there is a very powerful chapter of the Bible that is written about love. The kind of love in this chapter is a special love that only Christians can have. It is a love from God that flows through us. It is unconditional. It is loving like Jesus loves us.

⁴Love is patient, [1] *love is kind* [2] *and is not jealous;* [3] *love does not brag* [4] *and is not arrogant,* [5] *⁵does not act unbecomingly;* [6] *it does not seek its own,* [7] *is not* [8] *provoked,* [9] *does not take into account a wrong suffered,* [10] *⁶does not rejoice in unrighteousness,* [11] *but rejoices with the truth;* [12] *⁷bears all things,* [13] *believes all* [14] *things,* *hopes all things,* [15] *endures all things.* [16] *⁸Love never fails …*

1 CORINTHIANS 13:4-8A

Number the descriptions of love in the verses above. Put a "1" over patient, "2" over kind, etc.

"For us the combination of the Word, prayer, and the church have been lifelong parts of each day... These are the streams that God uses constantly to encourage us. We love the church! We encourage you to jump into your church family with both feet and love them. And if someone disappoints you, love them even more. As far as it depends upon you, try to always be in active fellowship with other Christians in your local community. Church is such an important part of your walk with Jesus."

- Ron and Marsha Harvell

Learning to Walk Daily With the Lord

QUESTIONS & REFLECTIONS

THE CHURCH
- ☑ God's Body
- ☑ God's Building
- ☑ God's Bride!

It is important to be a great church member. And greatness is defined as loving others with God's power. Ask your shepherd to help you with this. Follow the Holy Spirit's leadership in letting the church help you grow, help you serve, and help you be all that the Lord desires for you to be.

Write out a prayer of thanksgiving for your local church.

_____

_____

_____

_____

_____

Prayerfully consider who you could invite to attend church with you this week. Make a plan for connecting with them. Perhaps they could join you for coffee or a meal afterwards. Think about inviting your shepherd or some other people to connect with you and your friend after a service. This is a great way to make the connection more solid and for their visiting experience to have a more lasting effect.

Who can you invite to come to church with you this week?

_____

If they were to ask you why you attend or what you most enjoy about your church, what would be your answer?

_____

_____

_____

_____

Pray:

"Lord, You are in me. I am Your temple on the earth.
Holy Spirit fill my life with Yourself. I want to spur others on to love the church: Your Body, Your Building, Your Bride and encourage others on their journey. In Your name, Jesus, I pray. Amen."

"I love the church! I love being with God's people and growing and serving together with brothers and sisters in Christ. One of my life's pursuits is striving to be everything God designed the church to be."

- Todd Benkert

Week Six

WORSHIPING GOD

Come, let us worship and bow down,
Let us kneel before the LORD our Maker.

PSALM 95:6

LESSON OVERVIEW—WORSHIPING GOD

The theme of this week is **worship**. This lesson will be very straightforward and simple to teach. In the end, your lamb should grasp how important worship is to God.

Begin your time with prayer and answer any questions.

Spend time in your lesson, and then practice and encourage your student to worship each day in the way that they study. Make it sincere, even if it is uncomfortable. Worship is possible every day, and these truths can be practiced when alone, not just when in the company of other believers. However, corporate worship when you are together with other saints is an indescribable blessing!

Ask them their about their favorite Christian song or music. Share music that you love with them as well as ask them to introduce you to some worship music they have discovered.

- Their memory verses for this week will be—Thessalonians 5:16-18 and Romans 12:1-2.

- Have them share their memory verses from Week Five—1 Corinthians 3:16 and Hebrews 10:24-25

- Have them share their memory verses from Week Four—2 Timothy 3:16 and Psalm 1:1, 4-6

- These were their memory verses from Week Three—Matthew 6:9-13 (Optional 1 John 1:9)

- These were their memory verses from Week Two—John 14:15 and 21.

- These were their memory verses from Week One—Psalm 1:2-3.

- Answer any questions and allow them the opportunity to just talk with you.

- Provide an overview of Steps 37-42. Each of these days will increase their ability to be abke to worship God.

- Close in prayer.

Learning to Walk Daily With the Lord

DAILY PROMPTS FOR WEEK 6
STEPS 37-42—WORSHIPING GOD

Check in with your student each day to encourage them, to pray with them, and to continue developing your relationship with them. Here are some prompts that will help you as you connect with them each day.

STEP 37—TELL THEM YOU ARE PROUD OF THEM!

- Spend time in worship daily as you go through your lesson and encourage your student to do the same.

STEP 38—TALK TO THEM ABOUT WHAT COMES OUT OF THEIR MOUTH.

- This is a fun lesson—have fun with it!

STEP 39—ENCOURAGE THEM ABOUT THEIR THOUGHT LIFE.

- The mind is a battle ground. Reinforce how they can take their thoughts captive and use their minds to honor the Lord.

STEP 40—SPEAK WORDS OF LIFE TO YOUR STUDENT TODAY. BUILD THEM UP.

- Today's lesson spoke of presenting yourself as a living sacrifice. How we present ourselves to Him is

    1. Living (rather than dead).

    2. Holy (Jesus does this for us).

    3. Acceptable to God (right with Him through confessed sin).

STEP 41—TELL THEM YOU LOVE THEM.

- This is like a Valentine to the Lord—love Him with all your heart!

STEP 42—CELEBRATE HOW FAR THEY HAVE COME!

- Tell them what a great job they have done in coming this far in their journey.

- Allow them time to ask you questions or share with you.

- Prepare for Week 7 – Big Step 43.

Learning to Walk Daily With the Lord

☑ WEEK FIVE

STEP 36 — WORSHIPING GOD
INTRODUCTION

Welcome to Week 6! Isn't it great that God has given us Himself, Jesus, and the Holy Spirit so we can walk with Him forever? We pray that you can see how the Holy Spirit uses prayer, the Bible, and the church to help you in this glorious journey with Jesus.

Pray now and thank Him for all He has done for you.

What should we do for such an awesome God? You are going to dedicate time this week to learning how to worship God better. Worship is very important to God, and it is very important for you to worship the Lord all of your life.

A great way to study Bible verses, passages, chapters, or books is by asking Who, What, When, Where, Why, and How questions. Today your shepherd will walk you through these questions on the topic of worship.

1. Who to Worship?

Worship is mentioned 112 times in the Bible. In Exodus 20:1-5, God makes it clear that you are to worship only Him.

¹Then God spoke all these words, saying, ²"I am the LORD your God, who brought you out of the land of Egypt, out of the house of slavery. ³You shall have no other gods before Me. ⁴You shall not make for yourself an idol, or any likeness of what is in heaven above or on the earth beneath or in the water under the earth. ⁵You shall not worship them or serve them; for I, the LORD your God, am a jealous God…"

Mark every reference to God in the verses above. What do you learn about Him?

God spoke all these words: God is the LORD, God brought the people

out of slavery, You are to have no other gods before God,

The LORD is your God, He is a jealous God

2. What is Worship?

Worship is an act, thought, or expression of devotion that recognizes the superiority of someone or something. In the Old Testament, bowing down is very common. In the New Testament, the word worship means to bow down and throw kisses in adoration of the One being worshiped. Since God is the most important being in the universe, we worship Him. He does not like it when we worship anything or anyone else, so we bow down to, adore, and worship God.

3. When to Worship?

These three verses were part of your studies in Steps 4, 16, and 21. They are here again. They are also your first memory verses for this week.

16Rejoice always; 17pray without ceasing; 18in everything give thanks; for this is God's will for you in Christ Jesus.

1 THESSALONIANS 5:16-18

What are the time phrases? Put a clock over them.

Rejoicing is a form of worship. So is thankfulness, and talking to God is the most common, though certainly not the only, way to worship Him.

When should you worship God?

You should always worship God.

MEMORY VERSES

16Rejoice always;

17Pray without ceasing;

18In everything give thanks; for this is God's will for you in Christ Jesus.

1 Thessalonians 5:16-18

4. Where to Worship?

There are many who think you can only worship God in a holy place where He is residing or at a church service. But what does your memory verse from 1 Corinthians 3:16 tell you? You can worship God anywhere! Paul and Silas were worshiping God while in prison (Acts 16:23-26). Listen to this conversation between Jesus and a woman from Samaria (John 4:19-24):

19The woman said to Him, "Sir, I perceive that You are a prophet. 20Our fathers worshiped in this mountain, and you people say that in Jerusalem is the place where men ought to worship."
21Jesus said to her, "Woman, believe Me, an hour is coming when neither in this mountain nor in Jerusalem will you worship the Father. 22You worship what you do not know; we worship what we know, for salvation is from the Jews. 23But an hour is coming, and now is, when the true worshipers will worship the Father in spirit and truth; for such people the Father seeks to be His worshipers. 24God is spirit, and those who worship Him must worship in spirit and truth."

Underline "in spirit and truth." What does Jesus mean when He says you "must worship in spirit and truth"?

Worshiping in our spirit is the God-given ability to think about God and communicate with Him. It is the reason you can always be worshiping God. The Holy Spirit inside your spirit helps you do this. Worshiping in truth is worshiping God for who He is and what He does. These truths are based on God's Word and what the Lord is doing in your life and the lives of others.

50 STEPS WITH JESUS 103

5. Why Worship?
As you look at today's lesson, list why you think worship is important.

_____

_____

_____

6. How to Worship?
The rest of this week will be dedicated to teaching you how to worship.

Pray:

*"Lord, thank You that I know You and love You.
Help me to worship You this week!"*

STEP 37 — WORSHIPING GOD WITH YOUR BODY

Pray for the Lord to help you practice what you learn this week.

Since God is so creative and loves so much variety, it is not surprising that God likes to be worshiped in a variety of ways with your body. In the verses below, circle all of the ways you can physically worship God.

O clap your hands, all peoples; shout to God with the voice of joy.
PSALM 47:1

*Come, let us worship and bow down,
let us kneel before the LORD our Maker.*
PSALM 95:6

*Jehoshaphat bowed his head with his face to the ground,
and all Judah and the inhabitants of Jerusalem fell down before the
LORD, worshiping the LORD.*
2 CHRONICLES 20:18

*Therefore I want the men in every place to pray, lifting up holy hands,
without wrath and dissension.*
1 TIMOTHY 2:8

As you worship God today, select one of the ways of worshiping Him that you circled and worship Him that way. There is something significant in your worship of God when your body is modeling the humility or joy that your heart is expressing.

Write out your memory passage for this week, 1 Thessalonians 5:16-18, in the space below:

_____

_____

_____

_____

Be obedient to the Lord and practice doing what those verses say.

I can safely say, on the authority of all that is revealed in the Word of God, that any man or woman on this earth who is bored and turned off by worship is not ready for heaven.

—A.W. TOZER

STEP 38 — WORSHIPING GOD WITH YOUR MOUTH

As you start today's step, have fun with all of these ways to worship God with your mouth.

Pray:

> *"Lord, I want to worship You with my mouth."*

As you look at these seven verses, say them as prayers to the Lord.

For example:

> *His praise shall continually be in my mouth.*
> PSALM 34:1

You say to the Lord:

> **"Lord, let your praise continually be in my mouth."**

Now try it on your own:

> *He put a new song in my mouth, a song of praise to our God; many will see and fear and will trust in the LORD.*
>
> PSALM 40:3

> *O Lord, open my lips, that my mouth may declare Your praise.*
>
> PSALM 51:15

> *And my mouth offers praises with joyful lips.*
>
> PSALM 63:5

Learning to Walk Daily With the Lord

My mouth is filled with Your praise and with Your glory all day long.

PSALM 71:8

I will sing of the lovingkindness of the LORD forever; to all generations I will make known Your faithfulness with my mouth.

PSALM 89:1

With my mouth I will give thanks abundantly to the LORD; and in the midst of many I will praise Him.

PSALM 109:30

Wow! This is a powerful testimony of God's attributes. Now you are worshiping Him with your mouth by proclaiming the truths above.

How do your memory verses help you with the above prayers?

The verses in today's lesson are all talking about rejoicing in the

Lord always, praying to Him constantly, and being thankful.

STEP 39 — WORSHIPING GOD WITH YOUR THOUGHTS

Pray:

"God, help me worship You with my thoughts."

Today you will learn about worshiping God with your thoughts. Just like you use your voice to pray and sing to the Lord, you can also pray and sing in your mind. You are probably already doing this. In fact, this is the most common way believers communicate with the Lord. When you see a sunrise and think, "Wow God!" you are worshiping Him. You can talk to the Lord with your thoughts. This is how you can pray without ceasing.

You can also choose to have holy thoughts rather than unholy ones. Look at the verse below.

We are destroying speculations and every lofty thing raised up against the knowledge of God, and we are taking every thought captive to the obedience of Christ.

2 CORINTHIANS 10:5

You can take captive thoughts that bring doubt or thoughts that are wrong; you do not have to think them! God would not command us to take thoughts captive if it were not possible for us to do so. Pray and ask the Holy Spirit to help you. One way we take thoughts captive is to actively and intentionally replace negative or troubling thoughts with thoughts that honor God. Use the Bible verses you are memorizing to help you capture your thoughts.

Luke 10:27 tells us we are to love the Lord our God with all our mind. The only way to love Him with all our mind is to keep our thoughts engaged obediently to Christ.

These verses will help you see more ways you can worship the Lord with your mind.

Underline all of the items mentioned to meditate on:

*When I remember You on my bed,
I meditate on <u>You</u> in the night watches.*

PSALM 63:6

*¹⁵I will meditate on Your <u>precepts</u> and regard Your <u>ways</u>.
¹⁶I shall delight in Your <u>statutes</u>; I shall not forget Your <u>word</u>. ²⁷Make me
understand the way of Your <u>precepts</u>, so I will meditate on Your <u>wonders</u>.*

PSALM 119:15-16, 27

*On the <u>glorious splendor of Your majesty</u>
and <u>on Your wonderful works</u>, I will meditate.*

PSALM 145:5

There are two big thoughts here. The first is that you can talk to the Lord in your mind like you were connected to your best friend by phone 24-hours a day. The other is that you can worship the Lord by honoring Him in your thoughts. You can meditate on His greatness and deeds. Think about how wonderful He is!

Pray to the Lord with only your thoughts today. Even finish your prayer with "Amen."

Thinking the Bible verses you are memorizing and have already memorized is a great way to take your thoughts captive to the obedience of Christ.

STEP 40 — WORSHIPING GOD WITH YOUR ACTIONS

Now that you are worshiping God with your body, voice, and mind, you can discover a new way to worship. This is by living a life of actions dedicated to the Lord.

Pray:

"Lord, show me how to worship You with my actions."

Today you get two new powerful memory verses. They are Romans 12:1-2.

¹Therefore I urge you brethren, by the mercies of God, to present your bodies a living and holy sacrifice, acceptable to God, which is your spiritual service of worship. ²And do not be conformed to this world, but be transformed by the renewing of your mind, so that you may prove what the will of God is, that which is good and acceptable and perfect.

Mark the words "God," "you," "your," and the terms of conclusion ("therefore" and "so that"). What is God telling you in these verses?

Giving yourself to God as a living sacrifice is a way of worshiping

Him. He wants you to not be conformed to the world but be

transformed by renewing your mind to the things of God. Then

you can know God's good, pleasing, and perfect will for your life.

What are the three conditions for the sacrifice? (In other words, how do you present your body to God?)

1. Living
2. Holy
3. Acceptable

The "spiritual service of worship" is actually a phrase for Jewish priests who worked in the Jewish Temple. This means that when you serve the Lord with your life, you are worshiping Him! Notice that this is a living sacrifice. It is your life lived with the Lord.

Finally then, brethren, we request and exhort you in the Lord Jesus, that as you received from us instruction as to how you ought to walk and please God (just as you actually do walk), that you excel still more.

1 THESSALONIANS 4:1

When your life is dedicated to the Lord, this walk is an offering of your life, and it pleases God. Read these verses from Colossians 3:17, 23-24:

¹⁷Whatever you do in word or deed, do all in the name of the Lord Jesus, giving thanks through Him to God the Father. ²³Whatever you do, do your work heartily, as for the Lord rather than for men, ²⁴knowing that from the Lord you will receive the reward of the inheritance. It is the Lord Christ whom you serve.

MEMORY VERSES

¹Therefore I urge you brethren, by the mercies of God to present your bodies a living and holy sacrifice acceptable to God, which is your spiritual service of worship.

²And do not be conformed to this world, but be transformed by the renewing of your mind, so that you may prove what the will of God is, that which is good and acceptable and perfect.

Romans 12:1-2

Your actions for even routine parts of life can be an offering to God if you do them to honor the Lord. Combine your life being a living sacrifice, walking with the Lord, and doing work for the Lord into one package and you are worshiping with your actions!

Pray:

*"God, I commit my entire life to You as a living sacrifice.
I am holy through You. Help me walk with You and serve You
with the actions of my life."*

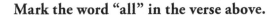

WORSHIPING WITH
MY ACTIONS:

☑ I am a living
sacrifice.

☑ I walk with the
Lord.

☑ I do the work of
the Lord.

STEP 41 — WORSHIPING GOD WITH YOUR HEART

Pray for the Lord to open your heart to Him in love.

Worshiping God with your mind and heart are important to Him. When you are in love with someone, your emotions drive your desire to express that love to them, to want to be with them, and to give yourself more deeply to them. There is no difference in how you should feel toward God. He loves you and wants you to love Him. Listen to Jesus describing the greatest commandment from Matthew 22:37.

And He said to him, "You shall love the Lord your God with all your heart, and with all your soul, and with all your mind."

Mark the word "all" in the verse above.

God wants you to love Him without reservations, without holding anything back, completely and wholeheartedly.

Read the following verses and draw a heart around the word "heart."

I will give You thanks with all my heart.
PSALM 138:1

*My heart is steadfast, O God; I will sing,
I will sing praises, even with my soul.*
PSALM 108:1

*The Lord is my strength and shield; my heart trusts in Him, and I am
helped; therefore my heart exults, and with my song
I shall thank Him.*
PSALM 28:7

50 STEPS
WITH JESUS   109

The heart expresses the joy and triumph of the Lord within the worshiper.

In the space below, write your heart's emotions to the Lord now that you are His child.

_____

_____

_____

_____

_____

_____

Pray to God, Jesus, and the Holy Spirit with your heart and mind. If you want to, kneel or raise your hands to the Lord as you talk to Him and tell Him how much you love Him.

STEP 42 — WORSHIPING GOD PUTTING IT ALL TOGETHER!

Pray and thank the Lord for this great week of learning how to worship Him with your life.

Today will be a review to help you remember the past 6 steps. Review your memory verses, 1 Thessalonians 5:16-18 and Romans 12:1-2.

List below a summary of what you learned about the 5 Ws of Worship on Step 36:

1. **Who to Worship:**

   We worship God alone.

   _____

2. **What is Worship:**

   Worship is an act, thought, or expression of devotion that

   recognizes the superiority of someone or something.

3. When to Worship:

We should always worship God.

4. Where to Worship:

We can worship God anywhere.

5. Why Worship:

We worship God because He is worthy of all worship. He is Lord of all. And He is seeking people who will worship Him in spirit and in truth.

What is your favorite way to worship with your body?

What did you say to the Lord the most this week with your voice?

What were your favorite thoughts of worship in your mind this week?

What difference did learning about worshiping with your actions make in your life?

_____

_____

_____

How did learning about how much God wants you to love Him yesterday make in your life today?

_____

_____

_____

Pray:

"God, help me to worship You with all I learned from this week. How exciting to adventure with You in learning to worship You with my ALL!"

SUMMARY

From Week 5 you have learned:

- **Step 29**—The Bible uses three great pictures to describe the church: the **body**, the **building**, and the **bride**. The word "church" means "called out assembly." As a Christian, you are part of the big global Church. Connecting to a local body of believers will help you grow and worship Him.

- **Step 30**—When you accepted Jesus as your Lord and Savior, you also accepted His Holy Spirit. The Holy Spirit now lives in you and empowers you to walk well with Jesus. He is the giver of spiritual gifts; He produces spiritual fruit in your life; He comforts, counsels, and abides in you.

- **Step 31**—We learned that there are 20 spiritual gifts listed in the Bible. They are listed here in alphabetical order:

1. Administration
2. Apostle
3. Distinguishing of Spirits
4. Evangelism (Evangelist)
5. Exhortation
6. Faith
7. Gifts of healing
8. Giving
9. Helps
10. Interpretation of Tongues
11. Leadership
12. Mercy
13. Miracles
14. Pastor
15. Prophecy (Prophet)
16. Service
17. Teaching (Teacher)
18. Tongues
19. Word of Knowledge
20. Word of Wisdom

- **Step 32**—All authentic Christians are saints to the Lord. By believing in Jesus, you have been made holy by His blood. Jesus is the foundation stone for your life just as He is the chief cornerstone of His Church.

- **Step 33**—The Church is the Bride of Christ, eagerly awaiting the glorious return of the Bridegroom. Just as a bride prepares carefully, the Church prepares herself to be presented to Him without spot, wrinkle, or blemish.

- **Step 34**—Joining a church family helps us connect meaningfully with other believers. This provides you with a vital link for strength, companionship, growth, and encouragement.

- **Step 35**—God's power allows you to love and serve others. Commitment to a local church helps you drink from one of the streams (Psalm 1) so you can bear fruit in season and never wither.

From Week 6 you have learned:

- **Step 36**—Worship is mentioned 112 times in the Bible. We learned that worship is very important to God. We meditated on Who, What, When, Where, Why, and How we worship our King!

- **Step 37**—We are to worship God with our bodies. Scripture is filled with ways to do this. Some of these ways are: clapping our hands, lifting our hands, dancing, kneeling, bowing, even falling on our faces before the Lord in reverence and in awe.

- **Step 38**—We are to worship God with our mouths. Some of the ways we do this is by singing, praying, and shouting praises with joyful lips.

- **Step 39**—We also worship God with our thoughts. We take wrong thoughts captive to the obedience of Christ. We meditate on His Word, think of His goodness, and focus our minds in gratitude and in praise.

- **Step 40**—Your actions for even routine parts of life can be an offering to God if you do them to honor the Lord. Combine your life being a living sacrifice, walking with the Lord, and doing work for the Lord into one package and you are worshiping with your actions!

- **Step 41**—We love God without reservations, without holding anything back, completely and wholeheartedly. This is how we love Him with all our heart, all our soul, and all our mind.

- **Step 42**—Worship is much more than an act we perform during church services or during special times of prayer or devotion. A lifestyle of worship takes time to develop. Worshiping God with all our life pleases God.

Write down two or three key things which have had the greatest impact on you the last two weeks of your journey.

_____

_____

_____

_____

_____

_____

_____

_____

Week Seven

Walking With Jesus As A Disciple

And Jesus came up and spoke to them saying, "All authority has been given to Me in heaven and on earth. Go therefore and make disciples of all the nations, baptizing them in the name of the Father and the Son and the Holy Spirit, teaching them to observe all that I commanded you; and lo, I am with you always, even to the end of the age."
Matthew 28:18-20

SHEPHERD'S GUIDE BIG STEP 43

LESSON OVERVIEW—WALKING WITH JESUS AS A DISCIPLE

Week seven is about **following Jesus as a disciple**. These are powerful themes to understand and do.

Begin your time with prayer and answer any questions.

The earliest Christians followed Jesus' teaching and leadership in their lives. They were behaving like Him. They were called Christians because they were acting like Him. He was in them through the Holy Spirit, and the people of Antioch were seeing Jesus through their outward actions.

The first call is to learn by being yoked to Jesus. They have probably been doing this already for six weeks. You have been a big part of the Lord's work in their lives. They should be able to walk with the Lord now on their own. This does not mean that they are completely self-sufficient; this means they can walk and talk with the Lord on their own.

The second call is to die to self. This is a refresher of Step 8. A true follower of Jesus will die to self and then live in Christ. This is an important principle to be able to say, "Not my will, but Yours be done." Abundant life in Jesus is a result of surrendering one's life and surrendering one's will to Him.

Finally, the Great Commission (Matthew 28:18-20) calls all believers to make disciples. In these verses, the words "go," "baptize," and "teach" are all words that find their focus on the main verb ..."make." As you go, make disciples by baptizing and teaching.

- Their memory verses for this week will be—Luke 9:23 and Romans 8:28-29.

- Have them share their memory verses from Week Six—Thessalonians 5:16-18 and Romans 12:1-2.

- Have them share their memory verses from Week Five—1 Corinthians 3:16 and Hebrews 10:24-25.

- These were their memory verses from Week Four—2 Timothy 3:16 and Psalm 1:1, 4-6.

- These were their memory verses from Week Three—Matthew 6:9-13 (Optional 1 John 1:9).

- These were their memory verses from Week Two—John 14:15 and 21.

- These were their memory verses from Week One—Psalm 1:2-3.

    - Provide an overview of Steps 44-49. Each of these days will increase their ability to walk with Jesus.

    - Really take seriously the closing prayer to the Lord as you pray together!

Learning to Walk Daily With the Lord

DAILY PROMPTS FOR WEEK 7
STEPS 44-49—WALKING WITH JESUS AS A DISCIPLE

Check in with your student each day to encourage them, to pray with them, and to continue developing your relationship with them. Here are some prompts that will help you as you connect with them each day.

STEP 44—CONGRATULATE THEM ON BECOMING AN AMBASSADOR.

- See if they have any questions from Step 43.

- Ask them how many times they must take up their cross (from their memory verse).

STEP 45—UNDERLINE THEIR POSITION IN CHRIST AS A BELIEVER.

- This is the "what they need to know to be saved" lesson.

- Ask if there is any question or if this brings them back to when they became a Christian.

STEP 46—ENCOURAGE THEM TO SHARE THEIR FAITH.

- This is the "what they need to do to become a Christian" lesson.

- Ask them who they know who needs to know Jesus as Savior.

STEP 47—REMIND THEM GROWTH IS ONGOING.

- Today's lesson shares powerful truths about God's power working in our lives and in the lives of other believers to mature us in faith. Share that we—none of us—are ever finished growing

STEP 47—ENCOURAGE THEM TO BE BOLD IN THEIR FAITH.

- Perhaps this would be a good day to have your student practice sharing their testimony with you as they would an unbeliever. You could role play and coach them through sharing the Gospel.

STEP 49—REMIND THEM THAT THEY ARE NEVER ALONE.

- Today provided a powerful set of promises from Jesus and how we are never alone. It was used as the last of their individual lessons just like Jesus promised in the last verse of Matthew in the Great Commission: "I will be with you always, even to the end of the age."

- Your student may be nervous about being on their own in two days. Assure them that they are never alone and that tomorrow on Big Step 50 you will work together on a plan for their ongoing growth in their walk with Jesus.

- Prepare for Big Step 50.

Learning to Walk Daily With the Lord

WEEK SIX

STEP 43 — WALKING WITH JESUS AS A DISCIPLE INTRODUCTION

Congratulations! You are starting the last week of this special journey. You have learned to walk with Jesus and worship Him. This week you get to learn the family business—helping others grow in their faith!

Pray and ask God to help you walk with Jesus every day of your life.

A disciple is a disciplined follower of a master teacher. A true disciple of Jesus is striving to be like Jesus. Soon after Jesus went to heaven, His disciples were called Christians (Acts 11:22). The disciples were following Jesus so well that they began to resemble the Lord, thus people started calling them Christians. The following three commands of the Lord will help you be a disciple:

1. Take My Yoke Upon You:

The Lord wants to help you walk with Him. In Matthew 11:28-30, Jesus calls you to join Him in His yoke. A yoke is a harness that helps animals pull wagons or plows together.

> [28]*"Come to Me, all who are weary and heavy-laden, and I will give you rest.* [29]*Take My yoke upon you, and learn from me, for I am gentle and humble in heart; and you shall find rest for your souls.* [30]*For My yoke is easy and My burden is light."*

While you are yoked with Jesus, He will teach you the things of the Father and things about yourself. As you journey alongside the Lord, you will learn, and you will find rest for your soul. What great promises for you!

The way you get yoked to Jesus is simple. You say, *"Lord, I want to yoke myself to You and learn from You and follow You."* Do this each day, and then listen and enjoy walking with Jesus.

2. Take Up The Cross:

Another call of discipleship is illustrated by the cross, and it is also a daily prayer. The call is found in Luke 9:23. This is your first memory verse for the week.

> *And He was saying to them all, "If anyone wishes to come after Me, he must deny himself, and take up his cross daily and follow Me."*

Just like the yoke required submission to the will of the Lord, the cross requires losing one's self in order to follow the Lord. The picture of the cross symbolizes a daily denial, often called dying to self, and a daily surrendering of one's will to the leadership of Jesus. This is a spiritual process and not a

DISCIPLE

A disciple is a disciplined follower of a master teacher.

physical one. Each day we find abundant life by dying to self and living for the Lord. Last week you memorized Romans 12:1-2. Quote these verses now.

When you present your life as a living sacrifice, you keep Jesus Lord of your life each day.

Jesus did the same thing. Before He was arrested and crucified, Jesus prayed in a garden outside of Jerusalem for God to choose a different way for salvation. Jesus knew that once He took all of our sins upon Himself He would be separated from God for the only time in His life. In this prayer He said, *"...yet not My will, but Yours be done"* (Luke 22:42). You must have this same attitude. A true follower of Jesus will answer His daily calls to join Him in the yoke and to die to self. You must put the Lord's will over your own, or it will hinder your growth. God's thoughts toward you are all good; His plans for you are always to give you a bright future filled with hope (Jeremiah 29:11). If you will trust His will for you, the result will be an abundant life filled with God's blessings!

3. The Great Commission:

One of those blessings will be participating in the mission of the Lord. These are the last words of Jesus before He ascended to heaven.

> [18]And Jesus came up and spoke to them saying, *"All authority has been given to Me in heaven and on earth.* [19]**Go** *therefore and* **make** *disciples of all the nations,* **baptizing** *them in the name of the Father and the Son and the Holy Spirit,* [20]**teaching** *them to observe all that I* **commanded** *you; and lo, I am with you always, even to the end of the age."*
>
> MATTHEW 28:18-20

Mark all the verbs in the bolded sentence starting with "Go" and ending with "commanded you."

How many did you find? <u>As many as 5 (depending)</u>

List them below:

<u>Some people will see these words as the verbs:</u>

<u>go, make, baptize, teach, commanded</u>

In the Greek language, there is only one verb. The others are a form of a verb that finds their identity in the main verb. The main verb is "make." The sentence could be written: *As you go, wherever you go, make disciples of everyone by baptizing them and teaching them.*

Once again, baptism is the most visible symbol of someone being a follower of Jesus. It represents salvation in this passage. As you go, make disciples by helping people become Christians and then help them be followers of Jesus.

Baptism is the most visible symbol of someone choosing to be a follower of Jesus.

This is your story. You are a disciple of Jesus. And someone is teaching you what Jesus taught His disciples. As you continue your journey in the Lord, you will help bring people to faith in Christ, and you will help others grow as new believers into maturity.

Let the weight of this build excitement in you. For the remainder of this week, you will walk with Jesus through each step and learn more each day about how to be a disciple maker.

Pray to the Lord:

"Dear Jesus, I want to walk with You in Your yoke and learn from You. Lord, I die to myself, to my will, and live for You as my Lord. I desire to help others come to know You and to follow You as Your disciples. In Your name, Jesus, I pray."

STEP 44 — WALKING WITH JESUS AS A DISCIPLE YOU ARE AN AMBASSADOR

AMBASSADOR

An ambassador is an official representative, one who promotes a specific activity.

As you think about how to be a disciple and a disciple maker, there are several important things to know and tools to help you with the tasks. The first is that you are an ambassador of the Lord. Pray for God to teach you how to represent Him to others.

The role of an ambassador as a diplomat is interesting. Ambassadors are a government leader's highest-ranking representative to a specific nation or international organization. They speak for that leader. They operate with their authority. They represent the interests of the one who sent them in word and in deed.

In this same way, you are an ambassador for Christ. You represent heaven's government and communicate God's extravagant love for the world by the One who sent you. Jesus gave you His authority (Matthew 28:18). When you speak, you speak for Him, so your words must reflect His heart of love to all who hear them.

Read this powerful set of verses from 2 Corinthians 5:17-20.

[17]Therefore if anyone is in Christ, he is a new creature; the old things passed away; behold, new things have come. [18]Now all these things are from God, who <u>reconciled</u> us to Himself through Christ and gave us the

ministry of <u>reconciliation</u>, [19]namely, that God was in Christ <u>reconciling</u> the world to Himself, not counting their trespasses against them, and He has committed to us the word of <u>reconciliation</u>. [20]Therefore, we are ambassadors for Christ, as though God were making an appeal through us; we beg you on behalf of Christ, be <u>reconciled</u> to God.

Underline the words "reconciliation," "reconciled," and "reconciling." They are found 5 times in these four verses.

Reconcile means to make right. If you owe someone something and have not paid them completely, then this exchange is not reconciled. Once it is paid in full, only then it is reconciled.

God used Jesus Christ to reconcile us to Himself. We needed to have the debt our sins created removed. Only Jesus could do that, and He did.

Find another phrase in verse 19 that has to do with debt. What does this mean to you?

<u>Not counting their trespasses against them</u>

<u>Thank You, God, for not counting my sins against me!</u>

God does not count our debts against us!

As believers we are both reconciled to God and given the ministry of reconciliation. This is how you are an ambassador for Jesus.

A big part of your new family's business is helping other people become Christians. You are representing Jesus to others. Don't worry. You do not have to do this alone since you are walking with Jesus.

We help move people toward a reconciled relationship with God by opening wide our hearts (2 Corinthians 6:11) and allowing God's compelling love to flow through us. He draws people to Himself; we simply share what He has done for and in us.

Pray:

"Lord, I open wide my heart for You to fill it with Your love. Flow through me every day. Please help me be a great ambassador for You among my family and friends!"

STEP 45 — WALKING WITH JESUS AS A DISCIPLE SHARING YOUR FAITH — PART 1

Steps 45 and 46 are tools for you to use to help others come to faith in Jesus. If available, your shepherd can share with you other tools your church uses to help others become Christians.

Pray:

"God, help me understand these two lessons so I can share my faith!"

Becoming a Christian is a big deal! It is the greatest day of a person's life. United with God—making Jesus Lord of your life—forgiven of sins— filled with the Holy Spirit. You become a new creation and get to be a child of God. It's a really BIG DEAL!

How to become a Christian is simple. There are a few things one needs to know and a few things one needs to do to become a Christian. Today you will learn what to tell people about becoming a Christian.

1. **God loves you and made you so that you can have a relationship with Him. When you become a Christian, you become a child of God.**

   See how great a love the Father has bestowed on us, that we would be called children of God; and such we are.
   1 JOHN 3:1

2. **To become God's child, you have to recognize that you do things that are wrong that separate you from God. These things that are wrong are called sin.**

   For all have sinned and fall short of the glory of God.
   ROMANS 3:23

3. **Sin caused a spiritual death in you.**

   The wages of sin is death ...
   ROMANS 6:23A

4. **Jesus came to the earth and died for you so you could have your sins forgiven.**

   ... but the free gift of God is eternal life.
   ROMANS 6:23B

MEMORY VERSE

And He was saying to them all, "If anyone wishes to come after Me, He must deny himself, and take up his cross daily and follow Me."

Luke 9:23

5. **In order to become a Christian, you must believe that Jesus is your Savior and Lord.**

> *⁹If you confess with your mouth Jesus as Lord, and believe in your heart that God raised Him from the dead, you will be saved; ¹⁰for with the heart a person believes, resulting in righteousness, and with the mouth he confesses, resulting in salvation.*
>
> ROMANS 10:9-10

As you read over these powerful truths, think about how much God loves you and how far you have come as a new believer! Meditate on this last verse–this is for you!

> *But God demonstrates His own love toward us, in that while we were yet sinners, Christ died for us.*
>
> ROMANS 5:8

Pray to the Lord a prayer of thanksgiving, again thanking Him for His love and salvation!

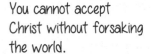

You cannot accept Christ without forsaking the world.

—A.W. TOZER

STEP 46 — WALKING WITH JESUS AS A DISCIPLE SHARING YOUR FAITH — PART 2

God's love is so powerful. As you share these truths with others, know that the Lord is doing amazing things behind the scenes to help them understand and to have faith. Each time a person becomes a Christian it is a miracle—someone dead is brought to life! The Holy Spirit has to be a part of every salvation. He is the One who is drawing them; He is calling them. You get to be a part of the process!

Pray:

> *"Lord, help me share with others how wonderful You are so they can know You."*

Step 45 taught facts you must believe for salvation. Today's step teaches actions of faith.

1. **It is not enough to know Jesus died on the cross and rose again from the grave. One must _ask_ God for forgiveness and _turn_ from their current life of sin. Part of confessing sin is a willingness to try not to sin anymore.**

> *¹²The Lord is Lord of all, abounding in riches for all who call on Him; ¹³for whoever will call on the name of the Lord will be saved.*
>
> ROMANS 10:12-13

If we confess our sins, He is faithful and righteous to forgive us our sins and to cleanse us from all unrighteousness.

1 JOHN 1:9

2. **One must also _acknowledge_ that Jesus is Lord. This is giving Him rightful authority over your life since He died for you and is Lord of all and King of kings.**

⁹If you confess with your mouth Jesus as Lord, and believe in your heart that God raised Him from the dead, you will be saved; ¹⁰for with the heart a person believes, resulting in righteousness, and with the mouth he confesses, resulting in salvation. ¹¹For the Scripture says, "Whoever believes in Him will not be disappointed."

ROMANS 10:9-11

3. **Another way to say this is: "_trusting_ your life to the Lord." This is the <u>step</u> of faith. It is like trusting a chair to hold you when you sit or like a child jumping into their daddy's arms without fear, knowing that the father will catch them.**

4. **Becoming a Christian is _believing_ that Jesus is the Savior, _seeking_ Him for forgiveness, and _giving_ your life to Him by _asking_ Him to live in you as your Savior and Lord.**

This simple prayer, if said with understanding and sincerity, is an example of how to ask Jesus into your life:

Dear Lord, I know that I am a sinner;
I know that You died on the cross and rose again
from the grave to forgive me of my sins.
I am sorry for my sins … Jesus, please forgive me of all of my sins.
Wash them away. I give You my life …
Please come into my life and be my Savior and my Lord.

Pray for someone you know who needs Jesus. Ask God to help them know Him and help you share this with them. An experience with Jesus Christ changes everything!

Who is someone in your life that God wants you to tell about Jesus? Write their name here and ask your shepherd to help pray for you and for them.

_____

SCRIPTURES FOR HELPING ME SHARE MY FAITH:

- ☑ I John 3:1
- ☑ Romans 3:23
- ☑ Romans 5:8
- ☑ Romans 6:23
- ☑ Romans 10:9-13

Look these Scriptures up in your Bible and underline them. You may want to write these references on the inside cover of your Bible for easy reference.

My friend, you could die holding the Bible and go to hell. Salvation does not depend upon head knowledge of the Scriptures. Salvation depends on heart experience of Jesus Christ.

—C.S. LEWIS

STEP 47 — WALKING WITH JESUS AS A DISCIPLE TEACHING OTHERS — PART 1

Pray and ask God to help you share with others what the Lord has taught you.

After helping someone become a Christian, the next part of making disciples is teaching them what the Lord taught His disciples. In other words, you need to teach others what the Lord has taught you. Once a person has encountered the Lord and become a Christian, they should become a disciple. Remember that a disciple is a disciplined follower of a master teacher. How well someone follows the Lord as a disciple is determined by the person's commitment to Jesus.

As you grow faithfully each day, you will become more like Jesus. Someday, when you leave this earth in physical death or when He returns to take you to heaven, He will finish your growth. You will be face to face with Jesus, and He will complete the work He began in you. Your last two memory verses are His promises:

28And we know that God causes all things to work together for good to those who love God, to those who are called according to His purpose. 29For those whom He foreknew, He also predestined to become conformed to the image of His Son, so that He would be the firstborn among many brethren.
ROMANS 8:28-29

Therefore, all Christians ought to be growing in their faith. This growth will result in you becoming more like Jesus. Everyone can mature more each day. Here is why:

As you join other Christians in practicing your spiritual gifts, you will help others grow ...

12... for the equipping of the saints for the work of service, to the building up of the body of Christ; 13until we all attain to the unity of the faith, and of the knowledge of the Son of God, to a mature man, to the measure of the stature which belongs to the fullness of Christ. 14As a result, we are no longer to be children, tossed here and there by waves and carried about by every wind of doctrine, by the trickery of men, by craftiness in deceitful scheming; 15but speaking the truth in love, we are to grow up in all aspects into Him who is the head, even Christ, 16from whom the whole body, being fitted and held together by what every joint supplies, according to the proper working of each individual part, causes the growth of the body for the building up of itself in love.
EPHESIANS 4:12-16

MEMORY VERSES
28And we know that God causes all things to work together for good to those who love God, to those who are called according to His purpose.

29For those whom He foreknew, He also predestined to become conformed to the image of His Son, so that He would be the firstborn among many brethren.

Romans 8:28-29

50 STEPS WITH JESUS

Learning to Walk Daily With the Lord

God has given us two hands. One to receive with and the other to give with..

—BILLY GRAHAM

It is important for each part of the church to build one another up and help each other. Jesus wants you to always learn. He also wants you to always help others learn and grow "…until we all attain … to the measure of the stature … to the fullness of Christ."

Think about these two truths from today. First, you are to always strive to grow to become more like Jesus each day. Second, the work of the church is not finished until everyone is complete in Christ. Therefore, both work together for the rest of our lives to help believers become more like Jesus.

Pray:

"God, help me grow every day of my life with my church and help me to disciple people well."

STEP 48 — WALKING WITH JESUS AS A DISCIPLE TEACHING OTHERS — PART 2

Yesterday you studied how all believers are to help one another grow in faith by building one another up in all aspects of church life.

When you accept the responsibility to serve others and help them in their walks with Jesus, it heightens your awareness of how you are walking. Ministering to others helps you grow as a disciple of Christ just as much as you are helping them to grow.

Today you will look at how focused teaching of an individual can help them grow rapidly in their faith. Just look at how much you have grown in the past seven weeks … now you get to help others grow as well.

Pray

"God, bring someone in my life or from my church that I can help to grow in their faith."

This type of small group or one-on-one disciple-making is very effective. It creates a cycle of simply helping others grow so they can help others grow.

As an illustration, examine what Paul said to Timothy, his beloved son in the faith:

*The things which <u>you</u> have heard from <u>me</u> in the presence
of many witnesses, entrust these to <u>faithful men</u> who will
be able to teach <u>others</u> also.*
2 TIMOTHY 2:2

Underline the four generations of discipleship. (Hint: Who did Paul teach? Who was he to teach? Who were they to teach?)

As you share with others the Lord's truths, you will find certain people who want to really know the Lord and walk with Him. Making disciples is helping those people walk with Jesus in such a way that they can, with the Lord's help, teach others how to walk with the Lord.

Is there someone God has placed in your life that you can share what you have learned over the past 7 weeks?

Who are you thinking of? _____

If no one comes to mind, ask your shepherd to see if they know someone or some ministry where you can share your life with others.

Pray and ask God to help the specific person or people that you are thinking about to grow in Jesus. Ask God to help you know how to teach them how to grow in their faith. If no one comes to mind, ask the Lord to bring people into your life that you can help shepherd or lead to Jesus!

List the four generations of discipleship from 2 Timothy 2:2.

1. _Paul (me)_

2. _Timothy (you)_

3. _Faithful men_

4. _Others_

Who are the believers helping you grow like Paul did for Timothy?

_____

Pause and thank the Lord for them.

STEP 49 — WALKING WITH JESUS AS A DISCIPLE JESUS IS WITH YOU ALWAYS

Pray:

*"Thank You, God, that You are in my life
and that I never have to be alone!"*

You have developed a relationship with Jesus over the past seven weeks. As a result, you know that He is with you. Today is a day of great encouragement because you will learn more about how faithful a friend Jesus is and how God is always with you!

50 STEPS
WITH JESUS   127

Mark the words "God" and "Jesus" in these encouraging verses from Romans 8:31-39. Underline the truths.

You may be living in a difficult situation. Christian, this is from God for you!

³¹What then shall we say to these things? _If God is for us, who is against us?_

³²He who did not spare His own Son, but delivered Him over for us all, how will He not also with Him freely give us all things?

³³Who will bring a charge against God's elect? God is the one who justifies; ³⁴who is the one who condemns?

Christ Jesus is He who died, yes, rather who was raised, who is at the right hand of God, who also intercedes for us.

³⁵Who will separate us from the love of Christ? Will tribulation, or distress, or persecution, or famine, or nakedness, or peril, or sword?

³⁶Just as it is written, "For your sake we are being put to death all day long; we were considered as sheep to be slaughtered."

³⁷But in all these things we overwhelmingly conquer through Him who loved us. ³⁸For I am convinced that neither death, nor life, nor angels, nor principalities, nor things present, nor things to come, nor powers, ³⁹nor height, nor depth, nor any other created thing, will be able to separate us from the love of God, which is in Christ Jesus our Lord.

As you inhale the Holy Spirit's encouragement, be even further encouraged.

Wherever you go in life for Jesus, He said:

"… **I am with you always,** even to the end of the age."
MATTHEW 28:20

If you doubt God's forgiveness, you have this promise of His faithfulness in 1 John 1:9:

If we confess our sins, **He is faithful** and righteous to forgive us our sins and to cleanse us from all unrighteousness.

If you wonder if you can approach Him in prayer, you have this truth:

²²Let us draw near with a sincere heart in full assurance of faith.
²³Let us hold fast the confession of our hope without wavering, for **He who promised is faithful**.
HEBREWS 10:22-23

As believers, sometimes we feel alone, but we are not alone—God is always with us! Sometimes we are tempted to doubt, but God never leaves us! Sometimes we still sin, but the God who is always with us will always forgive us!

He is so wonderful. He never asks you to do something that He will not help you with and be there with you the entire time. He is faithful! So as you take your steps through the Christian life, do them in step with Jesus! And **He** will always be with **You**!

Take a moment to write down some of the promises you read in the verses on page 102. For example: "You are with me, (your name), always, even to the end of the age."

_____

_____

_____

_____

_____

_____

Pray:

> *"Lord, thank You for Your faithfulness and always being with me!"*

_____
_____
_____
_____
_____
_____
_____
_____
_____
_____
_____
_____
_____
_____
_____
_____
_____
_____
_____
_____
_____
_____
_____
_____
_____
_____
_____
_____
_____

Week Eight

Celebration Day!

But as many as received Him, to them He gave the right to become children of God, even to those who believe in His name, who were born, not of blood nor of the will of the flesh nor of the will of man, but of God.

John 1:12-13

SHEPHERD'S GUIDE
BIG STEP 50

LESSON OVERVIEW—CELEBRATION DAY!
YOU COMPLETED YOUR 50 STEPS WITH JESUS JOURNEY

This is a celebration. Make this meeting special with a meal or a gift.

You should have four goals for this lesson:

1. Listen to their reflections on what they learned.

2. Give your reflections for them on how you see them. Provide lots of encouragement!

3. Define your future relationship. Are you open to helping them continue growing in the future?

4. Talk about what they do next in terms of growth and service in the church. There needs to be a path for them so they do not lose the momentum of the past 50 days.

You do not need to review them all, but here is a list of all their memory verses:

- Week Seven—Luke 9:23 and Romans 8:28-29

- Week Six—Thessalonians 5:16-18 and Romans 12:1-2

- Week Five—1 Corinthians 3:16 and Hebrews 10:24-25

- Week Four—2 Timothy 3:16 and Psalm 1:1, 4-6

- Week Three—Matthew 6:9-13 (Optional 1 John 1:9)

- Week Two—John 14:15 and 21

- Week One—Psalm 1:2-3

- Really celebrate how amazing they are, how hard they have worked, what they have learned, and how far they have come since they first began.

- Answer any questions and allow them the opportunity to just talk with you.

- Close in prayer, thanking God together for this remarkable journey!

Learning to Walk Daily With the Lord

STEP 50 — YOU COMPLETED YOUR 50 STEPS WITH JESUS JOURNEY REFLECTING AND PREPARING FOR THE JOURNEY AHEAD

Pray, thanking the Lord for this time you have spent growing with Him!

Do you not know that those who run in a race all run, but only one receives the prize? Run in such a way that you may win.

1 CORINTHIANS 9:24

Congratulations! You have finished this 50 step race and are now equipped to walk with Jesus for the rest of your life! Today you will get to write down some of the great things you have learned. You will also graduate into the next part of the journey.

As you look back through these past 7 weeks, what things did you learn about God, Jesus, and the Holy Spirit that you value most? Write them below.

_____

_____

_____

_____

_____

_____

_____

Spend some time in prayer thanking God for who He is and how much He loves you.

What are the three streams from Psalm 1?

1. Talking with God

2. Reading His Word.

3. Being part of His church

Looking back at Week 1, who are you in Christ?

You are a born-again child of God, an heir of God,

and a joint heir with Jesus. You are a new creation.

QUESTIONS & REFLECTIONS

Looking back at Week 2, what did you learn about obedience to Jesus? What were some of the ways you learned to follow Jesus?

Jesus is Lord. We must obey Him.

We obey and follow Jesus by being baptized,

taking communion, and telling others about Jesus.

We follow Him by loving and forgiving others.

In Week 3 we discussed prayer. What are the six types of prayer you learned about?

1. Thanksgiving
2. Praise
3. Confession
4. Petition
5. Praying for others
6. Conversational

During Week 4 you learned 8 tools to help you study the Bible. What are they?

1. keywords
2. lists
3. contrasts
4. comparisons
5. expressions of time
6. terms of conclusion, result, or purpose
7. paragraph themes
8. chapter themes

In Week 5 we discussed being part of the family of God through connecting to His church: His body, His building, and His bride. We talked about God giving us spiritual gifts—supernatural abilities—in order to serve others.

Think about what spiritual gift(s) you have discovered God has given you. What is it (are they)? How are you using these to serve the family?

_____

_____

_____

_____

_____

In Week 6 we focused on worship. Answer below the Who, What, When, Where, Why, and How questions.

Who do we worship?

We worship God alone.

_____

_____

What is worship?

Worship is an act, thought, or expression of devotion that

recognizes the superiority of someone or something.

_____

When do we worship?

We should always worship God.

_____

_____

Where do we worship?

We can worship God anywhere.

_____

_____

Why do we worship?

We worship God because He is worthy of all worship. He is Lord of all. And He is seeking people who will worship Him in spirit and in truth.

How do we worship?

We can worship with our body, mouth, thoughts, actions, and heart.

Last week (Week 7) we concentrated on sharing our faith with others. What key Scriptures did we learn that will help us share the path to salvation?

1 John 3:1

Romans 3:23

Romans 5:8

Romans 6:23

Romans 10:9-13

Looking back over all 50 Steps, what things did you learn about walking with Jesus that have helped you the most? Write them below.

As you prepare for the next part of your journey, you need to see this day not as: "I finished the race; now I get to rest," but as "I finished the preliminary race, and now I keep running into the next chapter of my walk with Jesus."

Therefore, since we have so great a cloud of witnesses surrounding us, let us also lay aside every encumbrance and the sin which so easily entangles us, and let us run with endurance the race that is set before us.

HEBREWS 12:1

As you mature in Christ, you should not feel alone. You have established an amazing relationship with Jesus. You have a shepherd who loves you. You have a church family who has embraced you.

What questions do you have for your shepherd about how you are to continue to grow and serve?

_____

_____

_____

_____

_____

_____

_____

_____

_____

_____

Write some words of encouragement for your student below.

_____

_____

_____

_____

_____

_____

_____

_____

_____

_____

_____

_____

_____

Pray together, thanking God for all that He has done and all that He will do in your walk with Jesus from now through eternity!

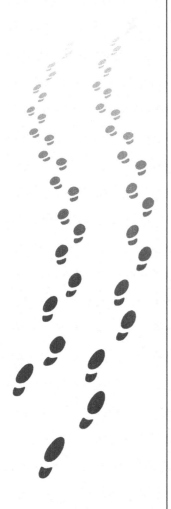

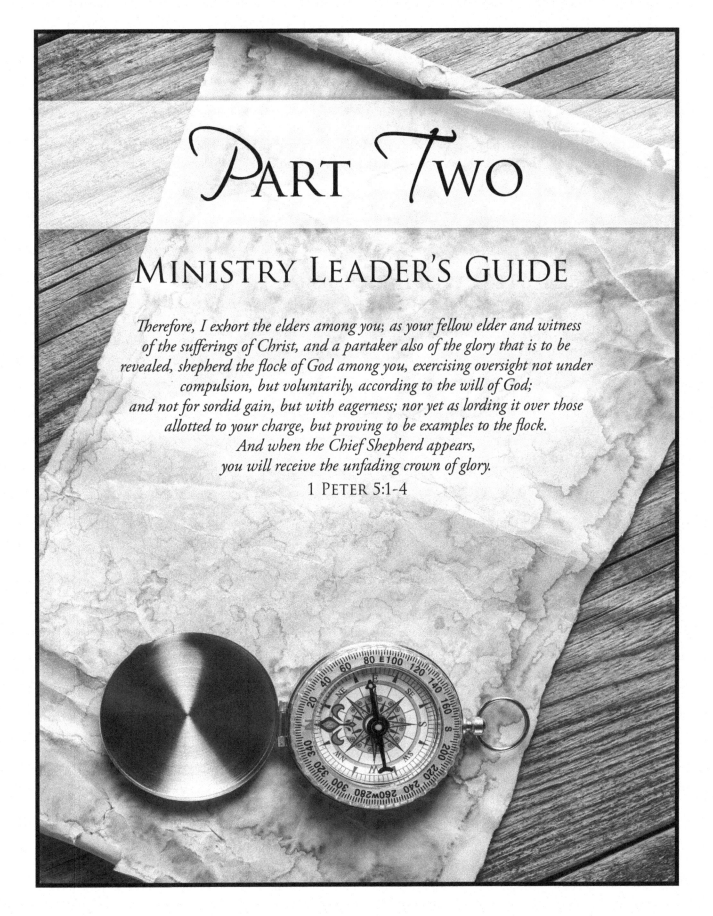

PART TWO

MINISTRY LEADER'S GUIDE

*Therefore, I exhort the elders among you; as your fellow elder and witness
of the sufferings of Christ, and a partaker also of the glory that is to be
revealed, shepherd the flock of God among you, exercising oversight not under
compulsion, but voluntarily, according to the will of God;
and not for sordid gain, but with eagerness; nor yet as lording it over those
allotted to your charge, but proving to be examples to the flock.
And when the Chief Shepherd appears,
you will receive the unfading crown of glory.*

1 PETER 5:1-4

WELCOME FROM PASTOR RON

Good day in the Lord, ministry leaders! Welcome to the Ministry Leader's Guide for *50 Steps with Jesus*. Marsha, Wendy, I, and most importantly—the creative leadership of the Holy Spirit—have developed *50 Steps With Jesus* to help nurture both new believers and any believer who wants to grow in their faith. Please look through these pages providing tools for leaders and prayerfully consider how your ministry would benefit from this journey tool and to what scale you would like to have your ministry participate.

WHAT IS *50 STEPS WITH JESUS* ABOUT?

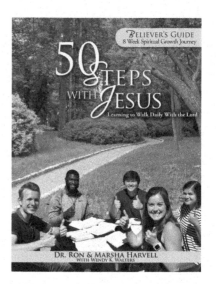

50 Steps With Jesus is a simple ministry tool to feed believers as they deepen their walk with the Lord. The results are profound as believers grow and learn the simple things of the faith, the elementary things, the milk.

For example, they learn:

- that Jesus really does love them.

- that He truly forgave them.

- that He wants to talk with them.

Believers finish their *50 Steps With Jesus* with a solid foundation for the rest of their Christian journey. The journey begins as if the believer is someone who has never prayed, opened a Bible, or been in a worship service. However, some students may have been believers for some time, but have never had the opportunity to develop these solid foundations in their walk with the Lord. The *Believer's Guide* was developed for the purpose of fostering intentional growth in each student's relationship with the Lord—

no matter where the "starting point" of their personal journey may be. Wherever they are beginning with the Lord, they will learn quickly from their guidebook and their experiences led by their shepherd. Their shepherd should take time to assess where they are, affirm what they already know, then fill in the missing gaps with each step.

The Lord's work through the shepherds is key to the success of this ministry. The shepherds lead believers who want to grow in their faith, on the *50 Steps With Jesus* journey. With the help of the Holy Spirit and their shepherd, the students are taught how to walk with Jesus using prayer, the Word, and the church. The shepherd meets with their believer face-to-face once a week and then makes daily contact every other day of the week.

Students use the *Believer's Guide,* and leaders use the *Shepherd's Guide.*

I am very excited about the potential of this ministry in the the lives of your flock. I have led many congregations through the years with many coming to faith and being baptized. We had programs for new members and a wide array of effective discipleship training for those who were already walking with the Lord. Yet, as I look back on my job as the senior shepherd of those flocks, I realize that I failed to nurture and train the new believers in their faith. I knew I needed to, but I was not prepared to intersect their lives with someone to help them grow starting the day of their salvation.

In speaking with many other pastors and ministry leaders, they confess to the same failure to help nurture the new Christians in their charge effectively. They instantly see the need for feeding these new lambs and want to have a practical, strategic way to tend the new believers in their churches. Some ministries have new member's programs, but very few have a new believer's ministry. Does your program have a way to intersect the lives of new believers and believers who would benefit from time spent on foundations with shepherds who will help them grow in their faith every day. We wrote *50 Steps With Jesus* as a tool to help leaders care for new believers by preparing "lamb shepherds" who are ready to walk with new believers during the early days and weeks of their Christian life.

WHAT IS THE BIBLICAL BASIS FOR A NEW BELIEVER'S MINISTRY?

Jesus's final words are very important to the writers of the Gospels and Acts. Each of these books has a commission from Jesus for the church. In John's Gospel, the Great Commission is found in a conversation between Jesus and Peter. The setting is on the shore of the Sea of Galilee. It takes place after Peter denied Jesus three times before the crucifixion, after Jesus' resurrection, and a few weeks prior to the Lord's ascension into heaven.

Peter needed to be restored and given purpose. Jesus restores Peter with three questions about Peter's love for Him. Following each of Peter's responses are three different commands. They are a charge to Peter to carry on the Great Shepherd Jesus' ministry for the flock. In the dialogue, the words for "tend" and "shepherd" are different. The word, "tend," means to feed. The word "shepherd" means to watch over and care for.

Jesus and Peter (John 21:15-17)

> *[15]So when they had finished breakfast, Jesus said to Simon Peter,*
> *"Simon, son of John, do you love Me more than these?"*
> *He said to Him, "Yes, Lord; You know that I love You."*
>
> *He said to him,* ***"Tend My lambs."***

[16]He said to him again a second time, "Simon, son of John, do you love Me?"
He said to Him, "Yes, Lord; You know that I love You."

He said to him, **"Shepherd My sheep."**

[17]He said to him the third time, "Simon, son of John, do you love Me?"
Peter was grieved because He said to him the third time, "Do you love Me?"

And he said to Him, "Lord, You know all things; You know that I love You."

Jesus said to him, **"Tend My sheep."**

Jesus' first command is to "Tend My lambs." I do not think it is accidental that Jesus also distinguishes "Shepherd My sheep" and "Tend My sheep." They are different. Jesus purposefully puts the lambs first. "Feed My lambs." Why are new believers' ministries not the most important ministries in the church?

Peter will later say in his letter to the church in 1 Peter 5:1-4:

[1]Therefore, I exhort the elders among you, as your fellow elder and witness of the suffering of Christ, and a partaker also of the glory that is to be revealed, [2]shepherd the flock of God among you, exercising oversight not under compulsion, but voluntarily, according to the will of God; and not for sordid gain, but with eagerness; [3]nor yet as lording it over those allotted to your charge, but proving to be examples to the flock. [4]And when the Chief Shepherd appears, you will receive the unfading crown of glory.

We, like Peter, are called to shepherd and feed the entire flock. This begins with caring for and feeding Jesus' lambs. A few principles drive the way *50 Steps With Jesus* was developed. They are:

- Just like any newborn human or animal needs immediate and consistent nourishment, a new believer needs spiritual food the moment they are born into the faith. In the *50 Steps With Jesus* ministry, you will be feeding (tending) and caring for new believers.

- Just like for any new living being, that early nourishment needs to be daily. Therefore, the ministry of tending your lambs ought to be with daily food and encouragement.

Please look through the materials for new believers and for shepherds to see how this ministry works. While ideally designed for one-on-one shepherding, this ministry can also be used in groups or for an entire congregation. Note the materials in "Why Is Involving And Training Your Congregation A Good Idea?"

Next up are training ideas for shepherds.

How Do I Select Lamb Shepherds And Train Them?

The selection and training of shepherds is important since they need to be ready and trustworthy. These ideas may seem to be commonsense, but we wrote them as a result of feedback from groups using *50 Steps* and from what we have seen work well. These are ideas for organizing and implementing *50 Steps With Jesus* into your ministries.

Shepherd Selection

- Lamb shepherds are selected based on their faithfulness and the confidence of the church leadership in them.

- Lamb shepherds are matched to lambs appropriately:

  - Women with women

  - Men with men

  - Children with parent or guardian present

    - If possible, shepherds for children should have a background check. The safety and protection of children is paramount If this is not available in your country, we strongly recommend that another adult is present in each face-to-face meeting between a shepherd and a child (or children).

- A church/ministry based tracking of lambs and their progress would help the shepherd be accountable and available, this could possibly be updated weekly.

- Develop a church/ministry based tracking of available lamb shepherds able to be updated as needed for best response to a new believer.

Shepherd Training

There is a training outline provided for you at the end of this section. The ideal situation would be to train a team of lamb shepherds who are ready to immediately help nourish the new believer beginning the day they come to know the Great Shepherd. To prepare for this:

- Walk your shepherds through the *50 Steps With Jesus Shepherd's Guide*.

  - The *50 Steps* ministry is plug and play in regards to simplicity.

  - Once shepherds go through the *Shepherd's Guide* and understand how the ministry works, they could immediately start helping others grow.

Learning to Walk Daily With the Lord

- Going through all *50 Steps* prior to being a shepherd is not required. We strongly recommend, however, that shepherds work through all *50 Steps* so that they know what the new believer is learning and what questions may arise.

- There are certain lessons on baptism, communion, and the ministries of the church where local input or doctrine can be provided to the shepherds as needed. The lessons are written broadly enough for the new believers to understand. Shepherds can teach the local church's doctrine and provide ministry opportunities as directed.

- The translation used in *50 Steps With Jesus* is the New American Standard Bible.

  - If your congregation or individual members use a different translation, you can encourage them to use their own Bible.

  - They can use their Bible translation for memorizing the memory verses in *50 Steps* if it differs from the NASB and is an acceptable translation for your church/ministry.

  - All of the exercises in *50 Steps* are accomplished using the Scriptures printed in the guides.

The people we have seen use *50 Steps With Jesus* understand the importance of this ministry. They catch how it works quickly. The shepherds are usually surprised at what they learn themselves and how much difference this makes in their life and the life of their lamb. We knew the daily contact was important, but we did not comprehend how powerful it was going to be in the new believer's life.

Learning to Walk Daily With the Lord

TRAINING OUTLINE FOR SHEPHERDS
This will require approximately 2 hours.

Session 1

As shepherds arrive, have a *Shepherd's Guide* and a *Believer's Guide* available for each shepherd.

In order to be able to track progress and maintain accountability, have each shepherd sign in with their name, contact information, and preferred group to work with (children, male, female, youth, etc.).

1. Start with prayer for the training.
2. Have them take out their **Shepherd's Guide**. Let them know that this may appear complicated, but it is simple in practice.
3. Have someone read **"The Adventure Begins"** (page 14).
    *   Ask the group to pray again silently for themselves.
4. Read **"The Purpose"** (page 14). Ask if it made sense and what their thoughts are on a new believer's ministry.
5. Teach **"The Great Shepherd's Command to You"** (page 15) and why it is important.
    *   Ask, "How does our church accomplish this ministry?"
6. Watch the Shepherd's Video.
7. Walk through **"Being A Good Lamb Shepherd"** (page 17).
8. Allow shepherds to ask questions and offer ideas.
9. Take a break.

Session 2

1. Explain to the shepherds again about <u>Big Steps</u> and <u>Daily Steps</u>.
2. Have them open **"Your Journey Map"** (page 7) to see how it is laid out on the contents page and on Steps 1 and 2.
3. Walk through **"Shepherd Preparation for Each Day"** (page 17).
4. Go over **"Principles for Meeting"** (page 18).
    *   Using the *Shepherd's Guide,* show how there is a lesson overview and prompts given to them to help prepare for each step, and how answers are also provided for them in their guide.
5. Discuss **"Ideas for Big Steps Weekly Meetings"** (page 19).
6. Discuss **"Ideas for 50 Steps Daily Contact"** (page 20).
7. Discuss **"Getting Ready for Week 1—Big Step 1"** (page 21).
8. Allow shepherds to ask questions and offer ideas.
9. Close with prayer.

WHY IS INVOLVING YOUR ENTIRE MINISTRY IN *50 STEPS* A GOOD IDEA?

Congregational Growth

Ministry and congregation-wide participation gives members the opportunity to understand *50 Steps With Jesus* through personal experience. This creates a church-wide enthusiasm for *50 Steps* and increases the pool of members who desire to be shepherds.

On a greater level, there is a personal growth benefit for everyone in the community who participates. People will grow as they teach or learn things that improve their own walk with Christ.

As an illustration, the earliest group to test *50 Steps With Jesus* was a group of believers in Colorado Springs. The group's average age was 70 years old, and the average time of being a Christian was over 50 years. They were amazed at the things they did not know. They all reported that they wished they had been taught how to walk with Jesus earlier in their faith.

One man said sadly, "Had I known how much Jesus wanted a relationship with me when I was 18, I would not have wasted 20 years of my Christian life."

Other reasons that leading this program for an entire congregation could be beneficial:

- Participants see the value in developing new believers.

- The spiritual maturity level of the congregation grows in Christ.

- Groups develop a greater sense of community and belonging.

Campaign

In order to create a congregation-wide or ministry campaign for your church, the following ideas and options can help supplement your plans in your unique environment:

- Have a season of prayer leading up to the launch.

- Prior to launch, preach or teach messages on the value of shepherding (Psalm 23; John 21:15-17; 1 Peter 5:1-4).

- Dedicate 8 weeks for doing *50 Steps With Jesus;* try to avoid competitive programs.

- Weekly sermons can be based on the Big Step themes discussed in steps 1, 8, 15, 22, 29, 36, 43, and 50.

- Implement the Big Step themes in all of your ministry groups for the weekly curriculum:
  - Small groups
  - Sunday school
  - Spiritual formation programs
  - Specialty groups such as women, youth, seniors, etc.

- The members would do their Big Steps in a group and then do the daily lessons on their own and be in contact each day with another member.
  - If possible have members sign-up to be either "New Believers/Students" or "Shepherds."
  - In some groups, people may want to practice being both.
  - In some small groups or families, three or four may be together contacting each other as shepherds and/or new believers/students.

- Have a celebration on the eighth week when you reach Big Step 50!

- Have participants who feel led to participate in ongoing shepherding sign up to become part of your lamb shepherd team.
  - If possible, have shepherds who will shepherd in specialties:
    - Children
    - Female youth
    - Female adult
    - Male youth
    - Male adult
    - Special needs

  - Develop a plan for usage that is common knowledge to the entire congregation so they know whom to contact for support of new believers.

WHERE CAN YOU GO FOR MORE ANSWERS? (FAQs)

Can we print this on our own?

You have permission in the front of these guidebooks to print as many as you need for your ministry, so long as they are not used for resale.

Can we modify the materials to fit our specific needs?

You are welcome to modify or add to these materials to meet the needs of your congregation. If you do a new language rewrite or insert your preferred translation, please let us know. We might be able to put it out on our website for others to use.

How do we contact you?

You can contact us at *GodsGreaterGrace.com* for the following:

- 50 Steps Training Videos
- Campaign Starter Video
- Ministry Updates
- A contact form to ask specific questions

Final Thoughts

Marie was the first lamb, and my wife, Marsha, was the first shepherd. Marie was a sergeant in the United States Air Force. She was not churched, but knew spiritually that she needed something more in her life. At the particular Air Force Base where she lived and worked, a small worship service was starting to reach her isolated neighborhood. Marie came to the worship services faithfully with her daughter. She became a Christian and was baptized on Easter.

Marsha asked her to go through *50 Steps With Jesus* with her. They met weekly, and Marsha texted Marie daily, in between their face-to-face meetings. Marie did not know about the Bible or about belonging to a local church, but she learned very quickly. Her countenance was one of joy as she loved Jesus and learned to walk and talk with Him throughout each day. We are so thankful to God that He laid this idea on our hearts and then sent Marie into our lives.

I join co-authors, Marsha Harvell and Wendy K. Walters, in our prayers that the Lord will richly bless you and your ministries as you feed well the lambs that God has given you. Have an amazing Journey!

Ron Harvell

For more information about this guide go to "The 50 Steps" section of our website, www.GodsGreaterGrace.com and click on the video, "Welcome to 50 STEPS WITH JESUS Learning To Walk Daily With The Lord."

You can contact us through the contact page as well.

WWW.GODSGREATERGRACE.COM

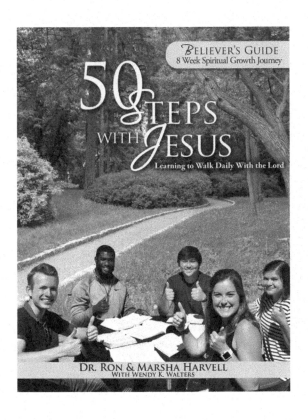

50 Steps With Jesus
BELIEVER'S GUIDE

The companion workbook to the *Shepherd's Guide*, the *Believer's Guide* is designed for the student to work side-by-side with you, the "shepherd," through each of the *50 Steps* provided in this 8 week course.

This guidebook is a tool created to help students on their journey with Jesus. Designed to be worked through with a shepherd for support and guidance, the *Believer's Guide* provides step-by-step instructions, key verses to memorize, and questions for growth and reflection.

Each day the student will take new steps with the Lord, exploring His truths, growing closer to Him, and becoming more secure in the foundations of the faith.

Is there someone in your life who God needs to make stable and steadfast in righteousness, truth, and holiness?

In Isaiah 62:6-7, God appointed watchmen on the walls of Jerusalem who never keep silent day or night. They constantly remind the LORD to establish Jerusalem. They refuse rest for themselves, and they will give God no rest until He establishes Jerusalem and makes her a praise in the earth.

God wants to establish you and your family. He invites you to be part of the establishment by praying for those He is establishing—become a watchman on the wall. Praying Scripture over your family allows you to pray God's Word in faith over any situation, unclouded and unceasing. As a faithful, prayerful watchman, you believe and stand in agreement for God's will to be complete in your family.

The Watchman on the Wall (Volumes 1 - 4) are a guide to pray God's Word daily and experience the joy of watching Him fulfill His promises. This will be an amazing year for you and those you love ...

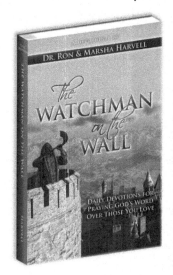
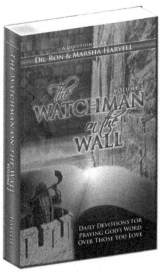
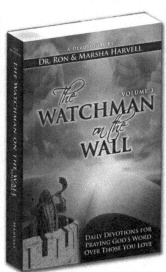
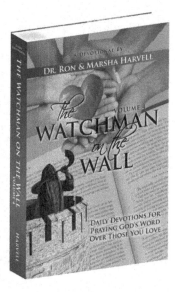

Available on amazon.com and GodsGreaterGrace.com.

What do sacrificing an animal, following Christ, and getting married have to do with each other?

COVENANT—It is a word that can sound academic and high church, yet it is the foundational concept for Who God is, and it undergirds all of Scripture.

Covenant weaves the Bible together. Covenant is the heart of God the Father. Covenant is the reason you can be in a relationship with Jesus Christ, and covenant is the foundation of every marriage. In *The Covenant Maker* you will:

Gain a richer knowledge of who God is, how you enter into a relationship with Him through Jesus Christ, and how God views marriage in light of covenant.

Change your way of thinking and increase your faith in God's faithfulness through knowing God and understanding covenant.

Available on amazon.com and GodsGreaterGrace.com.

How can you use your personality, natural gifts, talents, and developed skills to serve and glorify God?

Intentionality—Live on Purpose! helps you participate in the design of your own future. It will help you identify your passion and discover all that makes you unique, then guide you to focus your choices, your resources, and your energy on developing mastery in your field.

Many people feel they have been swept along by life's current. Learn how you can use your personality, natural gifts, talents, and developed skills to glorify God and live in joy. You can take the helm of your destiny and step into your unlimited future. You can begin to live fully engaged, fully alive—live with purpose ... on purpose!

Available on amazon.com and wendykwalters.com.

Made in USA - North Chelmsford, MA
1181126_9781735947709
10.12.2021 1055